all-time favorite
COOKIE
and baking recipes

your history

with Nestlé probably dates from when you were a kid snitching chocolate morsels while your mom baked cookies. Now, *Nestlé® All-Time Favorite Cookies and Baking Recipes* gives you the pleasure of sharing warm, freshly baked treats with your own family.

Like the famous no-fail Nestlé® Toll House® Cookies, these recipes, developed and tested in the Nestlé Culinary Center, guarantee batch after batch of sweet goodness year-round: drop cookies, bars, brownies, slice-and-bake cookies, pies, tarts, cakes and more. Best of all, you probably have the necessary ingredients stocked in your pantry.

Like you, generations of cooks have clipped the Nestlé® Toll House® Cookie recipe from its signature Nestlé packaging. This special book is filled with new and classic recipes that you can use for years to come. And look the other way when your children or grandchildren "steal" a few morsels. That's a tradition, too.

Left: Triple Chocolate Cookies (see recipe, page 33),
Choc-Oat-Chip Cookies (see recipe, page 32)
Right: Chunky Chocolate Chip Peanut Butter Cookies (see recipe, page 30)

contents

Celebrate the day with chocolate cakes, spice cakes and more.

Sink a fork into one of these homespun pies or elegant tarts.

Greet the morning with fresh-baked muffins or a hearty breakfast casserole.

The Nestlé® Culinary Center shares its secrets.

Pictured on front cover: Original Nestlé® Toll House® Chocolate Chip Cookies and variations (see recipes, pages 8-9)

Pictured on back cover: Craggy-Topped Fudgy Brownies (see recipe, page 70), Chocolate Macaroon Bars (see recipe, page 56) and Moist Brownies (see recipe, page 71)

Copyright© 2003 Nestlé USA, Inc. All rights reserved.
Produced by Meredith® Books, 1716 Locust St., Des Moines, Iowa 50309-3023.
Library of Congress Catalog Card Number: 20-03103287
ISBN: 0-696-21718-X Printed in the United States of America.

the legendary Nestlé®
Toll House® cookie

The Nestlé® Toll House® Cookie got its name from a lovely old tollhouse located between Boston and New Bedford, Massachusetts. Built in 1709, the house had long been a haven for weary travelers in search of food, drink and a change of horses.

In 1930, Mr. and Mrs. Wakefield purchased the historic old house and turned it into the now-famous Toll House Inn. In keeping with tradition, Mrs. Wakefield baked for her guests, perfecting and improving upon many old recipes. Soon, her tasty desserts attracted people from all over New England.

One day, while stirring together a batch of Butter Drop Do cookies, a favorite Colonial recipe, Mrs. Wakefield cut a bar of Nestlé® Semi-Sweet Chocolate into bits and added them to her cookie dough, expecting them to melt. Instead, the chocolate held its shape, softening to a creamy texture. This delicious discovery was dubbed the Nestlé® Toll House® Cookie, which became a widespread favorite. With Mrs. Wakefield's permission, Nestlé put the recipe on the wrapper of the Nestlé® Semi-Sweet Chocolate Bar.

As the popularity of the Nestlé® Toll House® Cookie increased, the company looked for ways to make this cookie easier to bake. First, Nestlé produced a special, scored chocolate bar that could be divided into small sections. Then the company began offering tiny pieces of chocolate in convenient packages—and that's how the first Real Nestlé® Toll House® Semi-Sweet Chocolate Morsels were introduced.

Since they were first created for the Nestlé® Toll House® Cookie, Nestlé® Semi-Sweet Chocolate Morsels have satisfied the chocolate cravings of millions. Today, they're used to make hundreds of delectable chocolate goodies all across America.

Original Nestlé® Toll House® Chocolate Chip Cookies and variations
(see recipes, page 8-9)

Lemon Sour Cream Stars

COOKIES:

  4 cups all-purpose flour, *divided*
  2 cups granulated sugar
  1 cup (2 sticks) LAND O LAKES® butter, softened
  ½ cup sour cream
  2 eggs
  1 tablespoon baking powder
  1½ teaspoons lemon extract
  1 teaspoon baking soda
  1 teaspoon vanilla extract
  ½ teaspoon salt

TOPPING:

  1 cup (6 ounces) NESTLÉ® TOLL HOUSE® Semi-Sweet Chocolate Morsels
  1½ teaspoons vegetable shortening

For Cookies:

BEAT 2 cups flour, sugar, butter, sour cream, eggs, baking powder, lemon extract, baking soda, vanilla extract and salt in large mixer bowl until well mixed. Stir in remaining flour. Divide dough into 4 equal portions; wrap in plastic wrap. Refrigerate for at least 2 hours or until firm.

ROLL out 1 dough portion on well-floured surface to ⅛-inch thickness. Keep remaining dough portions refrigerated. Cut with 2½- to 3-inch star cookie cutter. Place 1 inch apart on ungreased cookie sheets.

BAKE in preheated 350°F. oven for 8 to 12 minutes or until edges are lightly browned. Let stand for 2 minutes; remove to wire racks to cool completely. Repeat with remaining dough portions.

For Topping:

MICROWAVE morsels and vegetable shortening in small, heavy-duty plastic bag on HIGH (100%) power for 1 minute; knead. Microwave at additional 10- to 20-second intervals, kneading until smooth. Cut tiny corner from bag; squeeze to drizzle over cookies. Makes about 8 dozen cookies.

For Sour Cream Stars:

OMIT lemon extract; increase vanilla extract to 2 teaspoons.

cookies and candies

Recipe provided by Land O' Lakes, Inc.

Lemon Bars (see recipe, page 49), Lemon Sour C̶̶̶ Stars (see recipe, left) and Marbled Pumpkin Cheesecake (s̶̶̶, page 84)

Coconut Macaroons

1 package (14 ounces) or 5⅓ cups flaked coconut
1 can (14 ounces) NESTLÉ® CARNATION® Sweetened Condensed Milk
2 teaspoons vanilla extract
1 teaspoon almond extract (optional)

LINE baking sheets with foil; grease foil.

COMBINE coconut, sweetened condensed milk, vanilla extract and almond extract, if desired, in large bowl. Drop by rounded teaspoon on baking sheets lined with greased foil; press each cookie lightly with back of spoon.

BAKE in preheated 350°F. oven for 10 to 14 minutes or until lightly browned around edges. Immediately remove from baking sheets to wire racks to cool. Store loosely covered at room temperature. Makes about 4 dozen cookies.

For Coconut and Chocolate Macaroons:
STIR into dough ¼ cup NESTLÉ® TOLL HOUSE® Semi-Sweet Chocolate Mini Morsels. Prepare as directed.

The Milk from Contented Cows™

In 1899, E. A. Stuart and a partner founded the Pacific Coast Condensed Milk Company. Using the relatively new process of evaporation, the company offered sanitary milk at a time when it was not universally available. Stuart decided to name his product after a flower—the carnation—so children could easily remember the name. And so Carnation® Evaporated Milk was born. In 1907, the advertising slogan "The Milk from Contented Cows" was first used. Later, Carnation® Sweetened Condensed Milk was introduced. Over the years, both products have become cooking staples.

Butterscotch Apple Cookies

2½ cups all-purpose flour
 2 teaspoons ground cinnamon
 1 teaspoon baking soda
 ½ teaspoon salt
1⅓ cups packed brown sugar
 ½ cup (1 stick) butter or margarine, softened
 1 egg
 ½ cup apple juice
1⅔ cups (11-ounce package) NESTLÉ® TOLL HOUSE®
    Butterscotch Morsels, *divided*
 ¾ cup (1 small) unpeeled grated apple
 ¾ cup chopped walnuts, *divided*
    Butterscotch Glaze (recipe follows)

COMBINE flour, cinnamon, baking soda and salt in medium bowl.
Beat brown sugar and butter in large mixer bowl until creamy. Beat
in egg. Gradually beat in flour mixture alternately with apple juice.
Stir in 1½ cups morsels, apple and ½ cup walnuts. Drop by slightly
rounded tablespoon onto lightly greased baking sheets.

BAKE in preheated 350°F. oven for 10 to 12 minutes or until
lightly browned. Let stand for 2 minutes; remove to wire racks to
cool completely. Spread with Butterscotch Glaze; sprinkle with
remaining walnuts. Makes about 3½ dozen cookies.

For Butterscotch Glaze:
MELT remaining morsels and 2 tablespoons butter in small, heavy-
duty saucepan over lowest possible heat. Remove from heat; stir in
1 cup sifted powdered sugar and 1 to 1½ tablespoons apple juice
until smooth.

Crispy Polynesian Butterscotch Cookies

1½ cups all-purpose flour
½ teaspoon baking soda
½ teaspoon salt
½ cup (1 stick) butter or margarine, softened
½ cup vegetable oil
½ cup granulated sugar
½ cup packed brown sugar
1 egg
1 teaspoon vanilla extract
1⅔ cups (11-ounce package) NESTLÉ® TOLL HOUSE® Butterscotch Morsels
½ cup quick oats
½ cup crushed cereal flakes
½ cup flaked coconut
½ cup chopped nuts

COMBINE flour, baking soda and salt in small bowl. Beat butter, oil, granulated sugar, brown sugar, egg and vanilla extract in large mixer bowl until creamy. Gradually beat in flour mixture. Stir in morsels, oats, crushed cereal, coconut and nuts. Drop by rounded tablespoon onto ungreased baking sheets.

BAKE in preheated 350°F. oven for 10 to 14 minutes or until edges are crisp but centers are still slightly soft. Let stand for 2 minutes; remove to wire racks to cool completely. Makes about 3½ dozen cookies.

Pictured on page 22.

Frosted Maple Pecan White Chip Cookies

  3 cups all-purpose flour
  2 teaspoons baking soda
  2 cups packed brown sugar
  1 cup shortening
 ½ cup (1 stick) butter or margarine, softened
  2 eggs
  1 teaspoon maple flavoring
  1 teaspoon vanilla extract
  2 cups (12-ounce package) NESTLÉ® TOLL HOUSE® Premier White Morsels
 ½ cup chopped pecans
     Maple Frosting (recipe follows)
     About 60 pecan halves (3½ to 4 ounces)

COMBINE flour and baking soda in medium bowl. Beat brown sugar, shortening, butter, eggs, maple flavoring and vanilla extract in large mixer bowl until creamy. Gradually beat in flour mixture. Stir in morsels and chopped pecans. Drop by rounded tablespoon onto ungreased baking sheets.

BAKE in preheated 350°F. oven for 9 to 12 minutes or until light golden brown. Let stand for 2 minutes; remove to wire racks to cool completely. Spread with Maple Frosting; top each cookie with pecan half. Makes about 5 dozen cookies.

For Maple Frosting:
COMBINE 4 cups sifted powdered sugar, 4 to 6 tablespoons milk, ¼ cup softened butter and 1 teaspoon maple flavoring in medium bowl; stir until smooth.

Chocolate Peanut Butter Cookies

2¼ cups all-purpose flour

⅔ cup NESTLÉ® TOLL HOUSE® Baking Cocoa

1 teaspoon baking soda

¼ teaspoon salt

1 cup (2 sticks) butter or margarine, softened

¾ cup granulated sugar

⅔ cup packed brown sugar

1 teaspoon vanilla extract

2 eggs

1⅔ cups (11-ounce package) NESTLÉ® TOLL HOUSE® Peanut
Butter & Milk Chocolate Morsels

COMBINE flour, cocoa, baking soda and salt in small bowl. Beat
butter, granulated sugar, brown sugar and vanilla extract in large
mixer bowl until creamy. Add eggs one at a time, beating well after
each addition. Gradually beat in flour mixture. Stir in morsels.
Drop by well-rounded teaspoon onto ungreased baking sheets.

BAKE in preheated 350°F. oven for 8 to 10 minutes or until
centers are set. Let stand for 2 minutes; remove to wire racks to
cool completely. Makes about 5 dozen cookies.

*Chocolate Peanut Butter Cookies (see recipe, above), White Chip Island
Cookies (see recipe, page 20) and Oatmeal Scotchies™ (see recipe, page 120)*

Jumbo 3-Chip Cookies

    4   cups all-purpose flour
    1   teaspoon baking powder
    1   teaspoon baking soda
1½   cups (3 sticks) butter, softened
1¼   cups granulated sugar
1¼   cups packed brown sugar
    2   eggs
    1   tablespoon vanilla extract
    1   cup (6 ounces) NESTLÉ® TOLL HOUSE® Milk
        Chocolate Morsels
    1   cup (6 ounces) NESTLÉ® TOLL HOUSE® Semi-Sweet
        Chocolate Morsels
    ½   cup NESTLÉ® TOLL HOUSE® Premier White Morsels
    1   cup chopped nuts

COMBINE flour, baking powder and baking soda in medium bowl. Beat butter, granulated sugar and brown sugar in large mixer bowl until creamy. Beat in eggs and vanilla extract. Gradually beat in flour mixture. Stir in morsels and nuts. Drop by level ¼-cup measure 2 inches apart onto ungreased baking sheets.

BAKE in preheated 375°F. oven for 12 to 14 minutes or until light golden brown. Let stand for 2 minutes; remove to wire racks to cool completely. Makes about 2 dozen cookies.

White Chip Orange Cookies

2¼ cups all-purpose flour
¾ teaspoon baking soda
½ teaspoon salt
1 cup butter or margarine, softened
½ cup granulated sugar
½ cup packed light brown sugar
1 egg
2 to 3 teaspoons grated fresh orange peel
2 cups (12-ounce package) NESTLÉ® TOLL HOUSE® Premier White Morsels

COMBINE flour, baking soda and salt in small bowl. Beat butter, granulated sugar and brown sugar in large mixer bowl until creamy. Beat in egg and orange peel. Gradually beat in flour mixture. Stir in morsels. Drop by rounded tablespoon onto ungreased baking sheets.

BAKE in preheated 350°F. oven for 10 to 12 minutes or until edges are light golden brown. Let stand for 2 minutes; remove to wire racks to cool completely. Makes about 40 cookies.

White Chip Orange Cookies (see recipe, above), Double Chocolate Dream Cookies (see recipe, page 25) and Crispy Polynesian Butterscotch Cookies (see recipe, page 16)

cookies and candies

White Chip Chocolate Cookies

2¼ cups all-purpose flour
⅔ cup NESTLÉ® TOLL HOUSE® Baking Cocoa
1 teaspoon baking soda
¼ teaspoon salt
1 cup (2 sticks) butter or margarine, softened
¾ cup granulated sugar
⅔ cup packed brown sugar
1 teaspoon vanilla extract
2 eggs
2 cups (12-ounce package) NESTLÉ® TOLL HOUSE Premier White Morsels

COMBINE flour, cocoa, baking soda and salt in small bowl. Beat butter, granulated sugar, brown sugar and vanilla extract in large mixer bowl until creamy. Beat in eggs, one at a time, beating well after each addition. Gradually beat in flour mixture. Stir in morsels. Drop by well-rounded teaspoon onto ungreased baking sheets.

BAKE in preheated 350°F. oven for 9 to 11 minutes or until centers are set. Let stand for 2 minutes; remove to wire racks to cool completely. Makes about 5 dozen cookies.

The Best Cookies Ever

Here's a cookie jarfull of tips to help you turn out perfect cookies every time.

Baking sheets and pans of shiny, heavy-gauge aluminum bake cookies and bars more evenly than thin, dark metal or glass pans. Choose baking sheets that are the right size for your oven, allowing at least 2 inches of space between the sides of the baking sheet and the oven walls or door.

Grease baking sheets only when a recipe recommends it. Some cookies spread too much if the sheet is greased. When the recipe calls for ungreased baking sheets, cool and wash them between batches.

To prevent cookies from spreading too much on warm or humid days, spoon the cookie dough onto the baking sheets; chill the dough for a few minutes before baking.

For evenly shaped cookies, try a scoop. When a recipe calls for rounded tablespoons of dough, use a 1½-inch diameter scoop with dough leveled.

Butter and regular stick margarine work best for the recipes in this book (see Butter & Margarine, page 234). Also, all of the recipes were tested using large eggs.

To achieve the right oven temperature before baking, preheat your oven for about 10 minutes.

Bake cookies or brownies on the middle rack of the oven, one pan at a time, to prevent over-darkened bottoms and uncooked tops.

Check cookies and bars for doneness at the minimum baking time stated in the recipe. Remember, cookies continue to bake slightly after they are removed from the oven. For chewy cookies, take them out while they are still on the lighter side.

Let most cookies stand on the baking sheet for 1 or 2 minutes (or as long as directed in recipe) to continue cooking and to become firm enough to remove from the baking sheets. Then transfer cookies to wire racks.

Double Chocolate Dream Cookies

2¼ cups all-purpose flour
½ cup NESTLÉ® TOLL HOUSE® Baking Cocoa
1 teaspoon baking soda
½ teaspoon salt
1 cup (2 sticks) butter or margarine, softened
1 cup packed brown sugar
¾ cup granulated sugar
1 teaspoon vanilla extract
2 eggs
2 cups (12-ounce package) NESTLÉ® TOLL HOUSE®
   Semi-Sweet Chocolate Morsels

COMBINE flour, cocoa, baking soda and salt in small bowl. Beat butter, brown sugar, granulated sugar and vanilla extract in mixer bowl until creamy. Beat in eggs about 2 minutes or until light and fluffy. Gradually beat in flour mixture. Stir in morsels. Drop by rounded tablespoon onto ungreased baking sheets.

BAKE in preheated 375°F. for oven 8 to 10 minutes or until puffed. Let stand for 2 minutes; remove to wire racks to cool completely. Makes about 4½ dozen cookies.

Pictured on page 22.

Sensibly Delicious Chocolate Chip Cookies

    3 cups all-purpose flour
1½ teaspoons baking soda
    1 teaspoon salt
1¼ cups packed dark brown sugar
    ½ cup granulated sugar
    ½ cup (1 stick) margarine, softened
    1 teaspoon vanilla extract
    2 egg whites
    ⅓ cup water
    2 cups (12-ounce package) NESTLÉ® TOLL HOUSE®
        Semi-Sweet Chocolate Morsels
    ⅓ cup chopped nuts (optional)

COMBINE flour, baking soda and salt in medium bowl. Beat
together brown sugar, granulated sugar, margarine and vanilla
extract in large mixer bowl. Beat in egg whites. Gradually beat
in flour mixture alternately with water. Stir in morsels and, if
desired, nuts. Drop by rounded tablespoon onto lightly greased
baking sheets.

BAKE in preheated 350°F. oven for 10 to 12 minutes or until
centers are set. Let stand for 2 minutes; remove to wire racks to
cool completely. Makes about 5 dozen cookies.

*Sensibly Delicious Chocolate Chip Cookies (see recipe, above), Slimmer
Chocolate Crinkle-Top Cookies (see recipe, page 28) and Double Chocolate
Chip Brownies (see recipe, page 76)*

Slimmer Chocolate Crinkle-Top Cookies

  2 cups (12-ounce package) NESTLÉ® TOLL HOUSE® Semi-Sweet Chocolate Morsels, *divided*
1½ cups all-purpose flour
1½ teaspoons baking powder
  ¼ teaspoon salt
  1 cup granulated sugar
  2 tablespoons margarine, softened
1½ teaspoons vanilla extract
  2 egg whites
  ¼ cup water
  ½ cup powdered sugar

MELT 1 cup morsels in small, heavy-duty saucepan over lowest possible heat. When morsels begin to melt, remove from heat; stir. Return to heat for a few seconds at a time, stirring until smooth. Cool to room temperature.

COMBINE flour, baking powder and salt in small bowl. Beat together granulated sugar, margarine and vanilla extract in large mixer bowl. Beat in melted chocolate; beat in egg whites. Gradually beat in flour mixture alternately with water. Stir in remaining morsels. Cover; chill until firm.

SHAPE dough into 1½-inch balls; roll in powdered sugar to coat generously. Place on greased baking sheets.

BAKE in preheated 350°F. oven for 10 to 15 minutes or until sides are set but centers are still slightly soft. Let stand for 2 minutes; remove to wire racks to cool completely. Makes about 3 dozen cookies.

Pictured on page 27.

Mocha Biscotti

1½ cups all-purpose flour
½ cup NESTLÉ® TOLL HOUSE® Baking Cocoa
2 tablespoons instant coffee crystals
1 teaspoon baking powder
½ teaspoon baking soda
⅔ cup granulated sugar
3 tablespoons butter, softened
2 eggs
½ teaspoon almond extract
½ cup slivered almonds, toasted
1 cup (6 ounces) NESTLÉ® TOLL HOUSE® Semi-Sweet Chocolate Morsels

COMBINE flour, cocoa, coffee crystals, baking powder and baking soda in medium bowl. Beat sugar and butter in large mixer bowl until creamy. Add eggs and almond extract; beat until mixture is slightly thickened. Gradually beat in flour mixture; stir in almonds.

DIVIDE dough in half. With floured hands, shape into two 12-inch long rolls; flatten slightly. Place on one large or two small ungreased baking sheets.

BAKE in preheated 350° F. oven for 25 minutes or until firm. Cool on baking sheet(s) on wire rack(s) for 5 minutes. Cut into ½-inch-thick slices; arrange cut sides down on baking sheets. Return to oven; bake for additional 15 to 20 minutes. Remove to wire rack(s) to cool completely. Melt morsels according to package directions; drizzle over cooled cookies. Makes about 3 dozen cookies.

Pictured on pages 10-11.

Chunky Chocolate Chip Peanut Butter Cookies

1¼ cups all-purpose flour
½ teaspoon baking soda
½ teaspoon salt
½ teaspoon ground cinnamon
¾ cup (1½ sticks) butter or margarine, softened
½ cup granulated sugar
½ cup packed brown sugar
½ cup creamy peanut butter
1 egg
1 teaspoon vanilla extract
2 cups (12-ounce package) NESTLÉ® TOLL HOUSE® Semi-Sweet Chocolate Morsels
½ cup coarsely chopped peanuts

COMBINE flour, baking soda, salt and cinnamon in small bowl. Beat butter, granulated sugar, brown sugar and peanut butter in large mixer bowl until creamy. Beat in egg and vanilla extract. Gradually beat in flour mixture. Stir in morsels and peanuts. Drop by rounded tablespoon onto ungreased baking sheets. Press down slightly to flatten into 2-inch circles.

BAKE in preheated 375°F. oven for 7 to 10 minutes or until edges are set but centers are still soft. Let stand for 4 minutes; remove to wire racks to cool completely. Makes about 3 dozen cookies.

Pictured on page 2.

Choc-Oat-Chip Cookies

1¾ cups all-purpose flour
1 teaspoon baking soda
½ teaspoon salt
1¼ cups packed light brown sugar
1 cup (2 sticks) butter, softened
½ cup granulated sugar
2 eggs
2 tablespoons milk
2 teaspoons vanilla extract
2½ cups quick or old-fashioned oats
2 cups (12-ounce package) NESTLÉ® TOLL HOUSE®
    Semi-Sweet Chocolate Morsels
1 cup coarsely chopped nuts (optional)

COMBINE flour, baking soda and salt in small bowl. Beat brown sugar, butter and granulated sugar in large mixer bowl until creamy. Beat in eggs, milk and vanilla extract. Gradually beat in flour mixture. Stir in oats, morsels and, if desired, nuts. Drop by rounded tablespoon onto ungreased baking sheets.

BAKE in preheated 375°F. oven for 9 to 10 minutes for chewy cookies or 12 to 13 minutes for crispy cookies. Let stand for 1 minute; remove to wire racks to cool completely. Makes about 4 dozen cookies.

Pictured on page 2.

Double Chocolate Cookies

1¾ cups all-purpose flour

½ cup NESTLÉ® TOLL HOUSE® Baking Cocoa

1 teaspoon baking soda

2 cups (12-ounce package) NESTLÉ® TOLL HOUSE®
Semi-Sweet Chocolate Morsels, *divided*

⅓ cup butter or margarine, cut into pieces

1 can (14 ounces) NESTLÉ® CARNATION® Sweetened
Condensed Milk

1 egg

1 teaspoon vanilla extract

½ cup chopped nuts

COMBINE flour, cocoa and baking soda in medium bowl. Melt
1 cup morsels and butter in large, heavy-duty saucepan over lowest
possible heat, stirring until smooth. Remove from heat. Stir in
sweetened condensed milk, egg and vanilla extract; mix well.
Stir in flour mixture. Stir in nuts and remaining morsels (dough
will be soft). Drop by rounded tablespoon onto lightly greased
baking sheets.

BAKE in preheated 350°F. oven for 8 to 10 minutes or until
edges are set but centers are still slightly soft. Let stand for
2 minutes; remove to wire racks to cool completely. Makes
about 3½ dozen cookies.

Pictured on page 2.

Macadamia Nut White Chip Pumpkin Cookies

    2   cups all-purpose flour
    2   teaspoons ground cinnamon
    1   teaspoon ground cardamom
    1   teaspoon baking soda
    1   cup (2 sticks) butter or margarine, softened
    ½   cup granulated sugar
    ½   cup packed brown sugar
    1   cup LIBBY'S® 100% Pure Pumpkin
    1   egg
    2   teaspoons vanilla extract
    2   cups (12-ounce package) NESTLÉ® TOLL HOUSE® Premier
        White Morsels
    ⅔   cup coarsely chopped macadamia nuts or walnuts, toasted

COMBINE flour, cinnamon, cardamom and baking soda in small bowl. Beat butter, granulated sugar and brown sugar in large mixer bowl until creamy. Beat in pumpkin, egg and vanilla extract until well mixed. Gradually beat in flour mixture. Stir in morsels and macadamia nuts. Drop by rounded tablespoon onto greased baking sheets; flatten slightly with back of spoon or greased bottom of glass dipped in granulated sugar.

BAKE in preheated 350°F. oven for 11 to 14 minutes or until centers are set. Let stand for 2 minutes; remove to wire racks to cool completely. Makes about 4 dozen cookies.

Chocolate Mint Brownie Cookies (see recipe, page 36) and Macadamia Nut White Chip Pumpkin Cookies (see recipe, above)

Chocolate Mint Brownie Cookies

1½ cups (9 ounces) NESTLÉ® TOLL HOUSE® Semi-Sweet
      Chocolate Morsels, *divided*
1¾ cups all-purpose flour
 ½ teaspoon baking soda
 ¼ teaspoon salt
 ½ cup (1 stick) butter or margarine, softened
 ½ cup granulated sugar
 ¼ cup packed brown sugar
 1 teaspoon vanilla extract
 ½ teaspoon peppermint extract
 2 eggs
 ¾ cup chopped nuts

MELT ¾ cup morsels in small, heavy-duty saucepan over lowest possible heat. When morsels begin to melt, remove from heat; stir. Return to heat for a few seconds at a time, stirring until smooth. Cool to room temperature.

COMBINE flour, baking soda and salt in small bowl. Beat butter, granulated sugar, brown sugar, vanilla extract and peppermint extract in large mixer bowl until creamy. Add eggs, one at a time, beating well after each addition. Beat in melted chocolate. Gradually beat in flour mixture. Stir in remaining morsels and nuts. Drop by rounded tablespoon onto ungreased baking sheets.

BAKE in preheated 350°F. oven for 8 to 12 minutes or until sides are set but centers are still soft. Let stand for 2 minutes; remove to wire racks to cool completely. Makes about 3 dozen cookies.

Pictured on page 35.

Chocolate Peppermint Wafers

3 bars (6-ounce package) NESTLÉ® TOLL HOUSE® Premier White Baking Bars, broken into pieces

12 (about ⅓ cup) coarsely crushed unwrapped hard peppermint candies*

1 cup (6 ounces) NESTLÉ® TOLL HOUSE® Semi-Sweet Chocolate Morsels

1 tablespoon vegetable shortening

LINE 8-inch-square baking pan with foil. Line baking sheets with waxed paper.

MICROWAVE baking bars in medium, microwave-safe bowl on MEDIUM-HIGH (70%) power for 1 minute; stir. Microwave at additional 10- to 20-second intervals, stirring until smooth. Stir in candy.

SPREAD into prepared pan. Refrigerate for 10 minutes or until firm. Lift from pan; remove foil. Break into bite-size pieces.

MICROWAVE morsels and vegetable shortening in small, microwave-safe bowl on HIGH (100%) power for 1 minute; stir. Microwave at additional 10- to 20-second intervals, stirring until smooth.

DIP candy pieces ¾ of the way into melted chocolate; shake off excess. Place on prepared baking sheets. Refrigerate until ready to serve. Makes about 3 dozen pieces.

*Note: To crush candies, place in heavy-duty plastic resealable food storage bag; close. Crush with rolling pin or mallet.

Super-Easy Rocky Road Fudge

2 cups (12-ounce package) NESTLÉ® TOLL HOUSE®
   Semi-Sweet Chocolate Morsels

1 can (14 ounces) NESTLÉ® CARNATION® Sweetened
   Condensed Milk

1 teaspoon vanilla extract

3 cups miniature marshmallows

1½ cups coarsely chopped walnuts

LINE 13 x 9-inch baking pan with foil; grease lightly.

MICROWAVE morsels and sweetened condensed milk in large, microwave-safe bowl on HIGH (100%) power for 1 minute; stir. Microwave at additional 10- to 20-second intervals, stirring until smooth. Stir in vanilla extract. Fold in marshmallows and walnuts. Press mixture into prepared baking pan. Refrigerate until ready to serve. Lift from pan; remove foil. Cut into pieces. Makes about 4 dozen pieces.

cookies and candies

Rich Chocolate Pumpkin Truffles

2½ cups vanilla wafers (about 62 crushed)
1 cup ground, toasted almonds
¾ cup sifted powdered sugar, *divided*
2 teaspoons ground cinnamon
1 cup (6 ounces) NESTLÉ® TOLL HOUSE® Semi-Sweet Chocolate Morsels, melted*
½ cup LIBBY'S® 100% Pure Pumpkin
⅓ cup coffee liqueur or apple juice

COMBINE crushed cookies, ground almonds, ½ cup powdered sugar and cinnamon in medium bowl. Blend in melted chocolate, pumpkin, and coffee liqueur. Shape into 1-inch balls. Refrigerate. Dust with remaining powdered sugar just before serving. Makes about 48 truffles.

*FOLLOW melting direction on NESTLÉ® package.

bars and brownies

chocolate brownies and sinfully delicious bars tantalize young and old alike. Treat the kids to Chocolate Fudge Brownies while grown-ups nibble on Chocolate Amaretto Bars. Extra rich Outrageous Cookie Bars appeal to all ages. Let Chunky Pecan Pie Bars or Pumpkin Layered Bars grace your holiday table. Pan after pan, these bars are guaranteed to disappear quickly.

Swirled Peanut Butter Chocolate Cheeesecake Bars
(see recipe, page 58) and Outrageous Cookie Bars
(see recipe, page 60)

Banana Mini Morsel Bars

2 cups all-purpose flour
2 teaspoons baking powder
½ teaspoon salt
¾ cup (1½ sticks) butter or margarine, softened
⅔ cup granulated sugar
⅔ cup packed brown sugar
1 teaspoon vanilla extract
3 medium ripe bananas, mashed
1 egg
2 cups (12-ounce package) NESTLÉ® TOLL HOUSE®
   Semi-Sweet Chocolate Mini Morsels
Sifted powdered sugar

COMBINE flour, baking powder and salt in medium bowl. Beat butter, granulated sugar, brown sugar and vanilla extract in large mixer bowl until creamy. Beat in bananas and egg. Gradually beat in flour mixture; stir in morsels. Spread into greased 15 x 10-inch jelly-roll pan.

BAKE in preheated 350°F. oven for 20 to 30 minutes or until wooden pick inserted in center comes out clean. Cool completely in pan on wire rack. Sprinkle with powdered sugar. Cut into bars. Makes about 6 dozen bars.

Lemon Cheesecake Bars

CRUST:
- 2 cups all-purpose flour
- ½ cup powdered sugar
- 1 cup (2 sticks) butter

FILLING:
- 1 package (8 ounces) cream cheese, softened
- 2 eggs
- 1 can (5 ounces) NESTLÉ® CARNATION® Evaporated Milk
- ½ cup granulated sugar
- 1 tablespoon all-purpose flour
- 1 tablespoon lemon juice
- 2 teaspoons grated fresh lemon peel
  Yellow food coloring (optional)
- 1 cup sour cream

For Crust:
COMBINE flour and powdered sugar in medium bowl. Cut in butter with pastry blender or two knives until crumbly. Press into bottom and 1 inch up sides of 13 x 9-inch baking pan.

BAKE in preheated 350°F. oven for 25 minutes.

For Filling:
PLACE cream cheese, eggs, evaporated milk, sugar, flour, lemon juice, lemon peel and food coloring, if desired, in blender container; cover. Blend until smooth. Pour into partially baked crust.

BAKE at 350°F. for 15 minutes or until set. Cool completely in pan on wire rack. Spread sour cream over top; refrigerate. Cut into bars. Garnish as desired. Makes about 2 dozen bars.

Chunky Pecan Pie Bars

CRUST:
- 1½ cups all-purpose flour
- ½ cup (1 stick) butter or margarine, softened
- ¼ cup packed brown sugar

FILLING:
- 3 eggs
- ¾ cup light corn syrup
- ¾ cup granulated sugar
- 2 tablespoons butter or margarine, melted
- 1 teaspoon vanilla extract
- 1¾ cups (11.5-ounce package) NESTLÉ® TOLL HOUSE® Semi-Sweet Chocolate Chunks
- 1½ cups coarsely chopped pecans

For Crust:

BEAT flour, butter and brown sugar in small mixer bowl until crumbly. Press into greased 13 x 9-inch baking pan.

BAKE in preheated 350°F. oven for 12 to 15 minutes or until lightly browned.

For Filling:

BEAT eggs, corn syrup, sugar, butter and vanilla extract in medium bowl with wire whisk. Stir in chunks and pecans. Pour evenly over baked crust.

BAKE at 350°F. for 25 to 30 minutes or until set. Cool completely in pan on wire rack. Cut into bars. Makes about 3 dozen bars.

Creative Cuts

For flair with bars and brownies, cut them into shapes other than the standard rectangles and squares. To make triangles, cut bars into 3-inch squares, then cut each square in half diagonally. For diamonds, cut parallel lines 2 inches apart across the length of the pan, then cut lines 2 inches apart diagonally. For extra fun, cut less crumbly bars with cookie cutters.

Chocolate Chip Cranberry Cheese Bars

CRUST:
- 1 cup (2 sticks) butter or margarine, softened
- 1 cup packed brown sugar
- 2 cups all-purpose flour
- 1½ cups quick or old-fashioned oats
- 2 teaspoons grated fresh orange peel
- 2 cups (12-ounce package) NESTLÉ® TOLL HOUSE® Semi-Sweet Chocolate Morsels
- 1 cup (4 ounces) sweetened dried cranberries

FILLING:
- 1 package (8 ounces) cream cheese, softened
- 1 can (14 ounces) NESTLÉ® CARNATION® Sweetened Condensed Milk

For Crust:
BEAT butter and brown sugar in large mixer bowl until creamy. Gradually beat in flour, oats and orange peel until crumbly. Stir in morsels and cranberries; reserve 2 cups mixture. Press remaining mixture into bottom of greased 13 x 9-inch baking pan.

BAKE in preheated 350°F. oven for 15 minutes.

For Filling:
BEAT cream cheese in small mixer bowl until smooth. Gradually beat in sweetened condensed milk. Pour over hot crust; sprinkle with reserved flour mixture.

BAKE at 350°F. for 25 to 30 minutes or until center is set. Cool completely in pan on wire rack. Cut into bars. Makes about 3 dozen bars.

Lemon Bars

CRUST:
- 2 cups all-purpose flour
- ½ cup sifted powdered sugar
- 1 cup (2 sticks) butter or margarine

FILLING:
- 1 can (14 ounces) NESTLÉ® CARNATION® Sweetened Condensed Milk
- 4 eggs
- ⅔ cup lemon juice
- 1 tablespoon all-purpose flour
- 1 teaspoon baking powder
- ¼ teaspoon salt
- 4 drops yellow food coloring (optional)
- 1 tablespoon grated fresh lemon peel
- Sifted powdered sugar (optional)

For Crust:
COMBINE flour and powdered sugar in medium bowl. Cut in butter with pastry blender or two knives until mixture is crumbly. Press lightly into bottom and halfway up sides of ungreased 13 x 9-inch baking pan.

BAKE in preheated 350°F. oven for 20 minutes.

For Filling:
BEAT sweetened condensed milk and eggs in large mixer bowl until fluffy. Beat in lemon juice, flour, baking powder, salt and food coloring, if desired, just until blended. Fold in lemon peel; pour over crust.

BAKE at 350°F. for 20 to 25 minutes or until filling is set and crust is golden brown. Cool completely in pan on wire rack. Refrigerate about 2 hours. Cut into bars or triangles; sprinkle with powdered sugar. Makes about 4 dozen bars.

Pictured on page 13.

Chocolaty Raspberry Crumb Bars

CRUST:
- 1 cup (2 sticks) butter or margarine, softened
- 2 cups all-purpose flour
- ½ cup packed brown sugar
- ¼ teaspoon salt

FILLING:
- 2 cups (12-ounce package) NESTLÉ® TOLL HOUSE® Semi-Sweet Chocolate Morsels, *divided*
- 1 can (14 ounces) NESTLÉ® CARNATION® Sweetened Condensed Milk
- ½ cup chopped nuts (optional)
- ⅓ cup seedless raspberry jam

For Crust:

BEAT butter in large mixer bowl until creamy. Beat in flour, brown sugar and salt until crumbly. With floured fingers, press 1¾ cups crumb mixture into bottom of greased 13 x 9-inch baking pan; reserve remaining mixture.

BAKE in preheated 350°F. oven for 10 to 12 minutes or until edges are golden brown.

For Filling:

COMBINE 1 cup morsels and sweetened condensed milk in small, heavy-duty saucepan. Warm over low heat, stirring until smooth. Spread over hot crust.

STIR nuts, if desired, into reserved crumb mixture; sprinkle over chocolate filling. Drop jam by rounded teaspoons over crumb mixture. Sprinkle with remaining morsels.

BAKE at 350°F. for 25 to 30 minutes or until center is set. Cool completely in pan on wire rack. Cut into bars. Makes about 3 dozen bars.

Chunky Streusel Jam Squares

1½ cups all-purpose flour
1½ cups quick or old-fashioned oats
½ cup granulated sugar
½ cup packed brown sugar
1 teaspoon baking powder
¼ teaspoon salt
1 cup (2 sticks) butter or margarine
¾ cup raspberry or strawberry preserves
1¾ cups (11.5-ounce package) NESTLÉ® TOLL HOUSE®
Semi-Sweet Chocolate Chunks
¼ cup chopped nuts

COMBINE flour, oats, granulated sugar, brown sugar, baking powder and salt in large bowl. Cut in butter with pastry blender or two knives until crumbly; reserve ¾ cup oat mixture for topping. Press remaining oat mixture into greased 9-inch square baking pan. Spread preserves over crust; sprinkle with chunks.

COMBINE reserved oat mixture and nuts; sprinkle over chunks. Pat down lightly.

BAKE in preheated 375° F. oven for 30 to 35 minutes or until golden brown. Cool completely in pan until chocolate is firm or chill for 30 minutes to speed cooling. Cut into squares. Makes about 2 dozen squares.

Chocolate Marshmallow Mile-High Squares

2 cups (12-ounce package) NESTLÉ® TOLL HOUSE®
  Semi-Sweet Chocolate Morsels

1⅔ cups (11-ounce package) NESTLÉ® TOLL HOUSE®
  Butterscotch Flavored Morsels

½ cup creamy or chunky peanut butter

9 cups (16-ounce package) miniature marshmallows

1 cup dry-roasted peanuts

MICROWAVE semi-sweet morsels, butterscotch morsels and peanut butter in large, microwave-safe bowl on MEDIUM-HIGH (70%) power for 2 minutes; stir. Microwave at additional 10- to 20-second intervals, stirring until smooth. Cool for 1 minute. Stir in marshmallows and peanuts.

SPREAD into foil-lined 13 x 9-inch baking pan. Refrigerate until firm. Cut into squares. Makes about 2½ dozen squares.

Chocolate Crumb Bars

CRUST:

1	cup (2 sticks) butter or margarine, softened
1¾	cups all-purpose flour
½	cup granulated sugar
¼	teaspoon salt

FILLING:

2	cups (12-ounce package) NESTLÉ® TOLL HOUSE® Semi-Sweet Chocolate Morsels, *divided*
1	can (14 ounces) NESTLÉ® CARNATION® Sweetened Condensed Milk
1	teaspoon vanilla extract
1	cup chopped walnuts (optional)

CRUST:

BEAT butter in large mixer bowl until creamy. Beat in flour, sugar and salt until crumbly. With floured fingers, press 2 cups crumb mixture into bottom of greased 13 x 9-inch baking pan; reserve remaining mixture. Bake in preheated 350°F. oven for 10 to 12 minutes or until edges are golden brown.

FILLING:

COMBINE 1 cup morsels and sweetened condensed milk in small, heavy-duty saucepan. Warm over low heat, stirring until smooth. Stir in vanilla extract. Spread over hot crust.

STIR walnuts, if desired, and remaining morsels into reserved crumb mixture; sprinkle over chocolate filling.

BAKE at 350°F. for 25 to 30 minutes or until center is set. Cool completely in pan on wire rack. Cut into bars. Makes about 2½ dozen bars.

Swirled Peanut Butter Chocolate Cheesecake Bars

CRUST:
- 2 cups graham cracker crumbs
- ½ cup (1 stick) butter or margarine, melted
- ⅓ cup granulated sugar

FILLING:
- 2 packages (8 ounces each) cream cheese, softened
- 1 cup granulated sugar
- ¼ cup all-purpose flour
- 1 can (12 ounces) NESTLÉ® CARNATION® Evaporated Milk
- 2 eggs
- 1 tablespoon vanilla extract
- 1 cup (6 ounces) NESTLÉ® TOLL HOUSE® Peanut Butter & Milk Chocolate Morsels

For Crust:
COMBINE graham cracker crumbs, butter and sugar in medium bowl; press into bottom of ungreased 13 x 9-inch baking pan.

For Filling:
BEAT cream cheese, sugar and flour in large mixer bowl until smooth. Gradually beat in evaporated milk, eggs and vanilla extract.

MICROWAVE morsels in medium, microwave-safe bowl on MEDIUM-HIGH (70%) power for 1 minute; stir. Microwave at additional 10- to 20-second intervals, stirring until smooth. Stir 1 cup cream cheese mixture into chocolate. Pour remaining cream cheese mixture over crust. Pour chocolate mixture over cream cheese mixture. Swirl mixtures with spoon, pulling plain cream cheese mixture up to surface.

BAKE in preheated 325°F. oven for 40 to 45 minutes or until set. Cool completely in pan on wire rack; chill until firm. Cut into bars. Makes 15 bars.

Pictured on pages 42-43 and on page 61.

Chocolate Amaretto Bars

CRUST:
- 2 cups all-purpose flour
- 1 cup (2 sticks) butter or margarine
- ½ cup packed brown sugar

FILLING:
- 4 eggs
- ¾ cup light corn syrup
- ¾ cup granulated sugar
- ¼ cup amaretto liqueur or ½ teaspoon almond extract
- 2 tablespoons butter or margarine, melted
- 1 tablespoon cornstarch
- 2 cups sliced almonds
- 2 cups (12-ounce package) NESTLÉ® TOLL HOUSE® Semi-Sweet Chocolate Morsels, *divided*
- Chocolate Drizzle (optional; recipe follows)

For Crust:
BEAT flour, softened butter and brown sugar in large mixer bowl until crumbly. Press into greased 13 x 9-inch baking pan. Bake in preheated 350°F. oven 12 to 15 minutes or until golden brown.

For Filling:
BEAT eggs, corn syrup, granulated sugar, liqueur, melted butter and cornstarch in medium bowl with wire whisk. Stir in almonds and 1⅔ cups morsels. Pour and spread over hot crust.

BAKE at 350°F. for 25 to 30 minutes or until center is set. Cool completely in pan on wire rack. If desired, top with Chocolate Drizzle. Chill for 5 minutes or until chocolate is firm. Cut into bars. Makes about 2½ dozen bars.

For Chocolate Drizzle:
PLACE remaining morsels in heavy-duty bag. Microwave on HIGH (100%) power for 45 seconds; knead bag to mix. Microwave at additional 10-second intervals, kneading until smooth. Cut a small hole in the corner of bag; squeeze to drizzle chocolate over bars.

Pumpkin Layer Bars

¾ cup all-purpose flour

⅓ cup packed brown sugar

⅓ cup quick or old-fashioned oats

¼ cup chopped nuts

1½ teaspoons ground cinnamon

⅓ cup butter or margarine, melted

1¼ cups LIBBY'S® 100% Pure Pumpkin

1 cup NESTLÉ® CARNATION® Evaporated Milk

½ cup granulated sugar

1 egg

¾ teaspoon pumpkin pie spice

¼ teaspoon salt

4 ounces cream cheese, softened

¼ cup sour cream, at room temperature

2 tablespoons orange marmalade

COMBINE flour, brown sugar, oats, nuts, and cinnamon in medium bowl. Stir in butter, mixing well. Press into bottom of 9-inch square baking pan. Bake in preheated 350° oven for 20 to 25 minutes or until golden brown.

COMBINE pumpkin, evaporated milk, granulated sugar, egg, pumpkin pie spice and salt in medium bowl. Pour over oat mixture; bake at 350°F for 20 to 25 minutes or until knife inserted near center comes out clean. Cool completely in pan on wire rack.

COMBINE cream cheese and sour cream in small bowl. Stir in orange marmalade. Spread over pumpkin layer. Refrigerate. Cut into bars. Makes about 2 dozen bars.

Pumpkin Butterscotch Bars

COOKIE BASE:
- 1 cup all-purpose flour
- 1 cup quick or old-fashioned oats
- ¾ cup packed brown sugar
- ½ cup chopped walnuts
- ½ cup flaked coconut
- ¾ teaspoon pumpkin pie spice
- ½ teaspoon baking soda
- ¾ cup (1½ sticks) butter or margarine, melted

FUDGE:
- 2 tablespoons butter or margarine
- 1 can (5 fluid ounces) NESTLÉ® CARNATION® Evaporated Milk
- ¾ cup granulated sugar
- ½ cup LIBBY'S® 100% Pure Pumpkin
- 1½ teaspoons pumpkin pie spice
- ¼ teaspoon salt
- 2 cups miniature marshmallows
- 1⅔ cups (11-ounce package) NESTLÉ® TOLL HOUSE® Butterscotch Flavored Morsels
- ¾ cup chopped walnuts, *divided*
- 1 teaspoon vanilla extract

For Cookie Base:
COMBINE flour, oats, brown sugar, walnuts, coconut, pumpkin pie spice and baking soda in medium bowl; mix well. Stir in butter; mix well. Press into foil-lined 15 x 10-inch jelly-roll pan.

BAKE in 350°F. oven for 13 to 15 minutes or until slightly brown. Cool completely in pan on wire rack.

For Fudge:
COMBINE butter, evaporated milk, granulated sugar, pumpkin, pumpkin pie spice and salt in medium, heavy-duty saucepan. Bring to a boil, stirring constantly, over medium heat. Boil, stirring constantly, for 8 to 10 minutes. Remove from heat.

STIR in marshmallows, morsels, ½ cup walnuts and vanilla extract. Stir vigorously for 1 minute or until marshmallows are melted. Pour over cookie base; sprinkle with remaining walnuts. Refrigerate until firm. Cut into bars. Makes about 4 dozen bars.

Pictured on page 67.

Date Bars

1 package (8 ounces) chopped dates
¾ cup NESTLÉ® CARNATION® Evaporated Milk
2 tablespoons granulated sugar
1 teaspoon vanilla extract
½ cup (1 stick) butter or margarine, softened
½ cup packed light brown sugar
1 cup all-purpose flour
¾ cup quick-cooking oats
½ teaspoon baking soda
½ teaspoon salt
½ teaspoon ground cinnamon

COMBINE dates, evaporated milk, granulated sugar and vanilla extract in medium saucepan. Cook over medium-low heat, stirring occasionally, for 8 to 10 minutes or until thickened. Remove from heat.

BEAT butter and brown sugar in large mixer bowl until creamy. Beat in flour, oats, baking soda, salt and cinnamon. With floured fingers, press half of crust mixture into bottom of greased 8-inch square baking dish. Spread date filling over crust. Top with remaining crust.

BAKE in preheated 400°F. oven for 20 to 25 minutes or until golden. Cut into bars. Serve warm. Makes 16 bars.

Date Bars (see recipe, above) and Pumpkin Butterscotch Bars (see recipe, page 65)

In-the-Pan Brownies

½ cup (1 stick) butter
2 cups granulated sugar
1 cup all-purpose flour
1 cup chopped pecans
4 eggs
4 packets (1 ounce each) NESTLÉ® TOLL HOUSE® CHOCO
BAKE® Unsweetened Chocolate Flavor
1 teaspoon vanilla extract
¼ teaspoon ground cinnamon

MELT butter in 13 x 9-inch baking pan in preheated 350°F. oven;
remove from oven. Stir in sugar, flour, pecans, eggs, Choco Bake,
vanilla extract and cinnamon with a fork until well blended.
Smooth batter with spatula.

BAKE at 350°F. for 25 to 30 minutes or until wooden pick inserted
in center comes out clean. Cool completely in pan on wire rack.
Cut into bars. Makes 28 brownies.

Chocolate Fudge Brownies

1⅔ cups granulated sugar

½ cup (1 stick) butter or margarine

2 tablespoons water

2 bars (2 ounces each) NESTLÉ® TOLL HOUSE® Unsweetened Baking Chocolate, broken into pieces

2 eggs

1½ teaspoons vanilla extract

1⅓ cups all-purpose flour

¼ teaspoon baking soda

¼ teaspoon salt

½ cup chopped nuts (optional)

MICROWAVE sugar, butter and water in large, microwave-safe bowl on HIGH (100%) power for 4 to 5 minutes or until mixture bubbles, stirring once. (Or, heat granulated sugar, butter and water in medium saucepan just to boiling, stirring constantly. Remove from heat.) Add baking bars, stirring until melted.

STIR in eggs, one at a time, beating well after each addition. Stir in vanilla extract. Gradually stir in flour, baking soda and salt. If desired, stir in nuts. Pour into greased 13 x 9-inch baking pan.

BAKE in preheated 350°F. oven for 15 to 20 minutes or until wooden pick inserted in center comes out slightly sticky. Cool completely in pan on wire rack. Cut into bars. Makes about 2 dozen brownies.

Peanut Butter Brownie Variation:

PREPARE batter as above without nuts; do not pour into pan. Combine ½ cup creamy or chunky peanut butter, 3 tablespoons granulated sugar and 2 tablespoons milk in medium, microwave-safe bowl. Microwave on HIGH (100%) power for 45 seconds; stir until smooth. Pour batter into pan. Spoon peanut butter mixture over top; swirl with spoon. Bake in preheated 350°F. oven for 20 to 25 minutes. Cool completely in pan on wire rack. Cut into bars.

Craggy-Topped Fudge Brownies

  1 cup granulated sugar
 ½ cup (1 stick) butter or margarine
  2 cups (12-ounce package) NESTLÉ® TOLL HOUSE®
      Semi-Sweet Chocolate Morsels, *divided*
  3 eggs
1⅓ cups all-purpose flour
  1 teaspoon vanilla extract
 ¼ teaspoon baking soda
 ⅓ cup chopped nuts

HEAT sugar and butter in medium saucepan over low heat, stirring until butter is melted. Remove from heat. Add 1¼ cups morsels; stir until melted. Stir in eggs. Stir in flour, vanilla extract and baking soda until combined. Spread into greased 13 x 9-inch baking pan.

BAKE in preheated 350°F. oven for 18 to 22 minutes or until wooden pick inserted in center comes out slightly sticky.

SPRINKLE with remaining morsels and nuts while still hot. Cover with foil; refrigerate in pan until completely cooled. Cut into bars. Makes about 2 dozen brownies.

Pictured on page 57.

Moist Brownies

BROWNIES:

1¼ cups all-purpose flour

½ teaspoon baking soda

¼ teaspoon salt

¾ cup granulated sugar

½ cup (1 stick) butter or margarine

2 tablespoons water

1½ cups (9 ounces) NESTLÉ® TOLL HOUSE® Semi-Sweet
    Chocolate Morsels, *divided*

1 teaspoon vanilla extract

2 eggs

FROSTING:

1 container (16 ounces) prepared vanilla frosting

1 tube (4¼ ounces) chocolate decorating icing

For Brownies:

COMBINE flour, baking soda and salt in small bowl. Combine sugar, butter and water in medium saucepan. Bring just to a boil over medium heat, stirring constantly; remove from heat. (Or combine sugar, butter and water in medium, microwave-safe bowl. Microwave on HIGH [100%] power for 3 minutes, stirring halfway through cooking time. Stir until smooth.)

ADD 1 cup morsels and vanilla extract; stir until smooth. Add eggs, one at a time, stirring well after each addition. Stir in flour mixture and remaining morsels. Spread into greased 9-inch square baking pan.

BAKE in preheated 350°F. oven for 20 to 30 minutes or until center is set. Cool completely (center will sink) in pan on rack.

For Frosting:

SPREAD vanilla frosting over brownies. Squeeze chocolate icing in parallel lines over frosting. Drag wooden pick through chocolate icing to feather. Let stand until frosting is set. Cut into bars. Makes 16 brownies.

Pictured on page 57.

Chocolate Turtle Brownies

2 cups (12-ounce package) NESTLÉ® TOLL HOUSE®
Semi-Sweet Chocolate Morsels, *divided*

½ cup (1 stick) butter or margarine, cut into pieces

3 eggs

1¼ cups all-purpose flour

1 cup granulated sugar

1 teaspoon vanilla extract

¼ teaspoon baking soda

½ cup chopped walnuts

12 caramels, unwrapped

1 tablespoon milk

MELT 1 cup morsels and butter in large, heavy-duty saucepan over lowest possible heat, stirring constantly until smooth. Remove from heat; stir in eggs. Add flour, sugar, vanilla extract and baking soda; stir well. Spread batter into greased 13 x 9-inch baking pan; sprinkle with remaining morsels and walnuts.

BAKE in preheated 350°F. oven for 20 to 25 minutes or until wooden pick inserted in center comes out slightly sticky.

MICROWAVE caramels and milk in small, microwave-safe bowl on HIGH (100%) power for 1 minute; stir. Microwave at additional 10- to 20-second intervals, stirring until smooth. Drizzle over warm brownies. Cool completely in pan on wire rack. Cut into bars. Makes about 2 dozen brownies.

German Chocolate Brownies

1 package (18½ ounces) chocolate cake mix
1 cup chopped nuts
½ cup (1 stick) butter or margarine, melted
1 cup NESTLÉ® CARNATION® Evaporated Milk, *divided*
35 (10-ounce package) caramels, unwrapped
2 cups (12-ounce package) NESTLÉ® TOLL HOUSE®
Semi-Sweet Chocolate Morsels

COMBINE cake mix and nuts in large bowl. Stir in butter. Stir in ⅔ cup evaporated milk (batter will be thick). Spread half of batter into ungreased 13 x 9-inch baking pan. Bake in preheated 350°F. oven for 15 minutes.

COOK caramels and remaining evaporated milk in small saucepan over low heat, stirring constantly until caramels are melted. Sprinkle morsels over hot base; drizzle with caramel mixture.

DROP remaining batter by heaping teaspoon over caramel mixture. Bake at 350°F. for 25 to 30 minutes or until center is set. Cool completely in pan on wire rack. Cut into bars. Makes about 4 dozen brownies.

Frosted Brownies

BROWNIES:

- ⅔ cup all-purpose flour
- ½ teaspoon baking powder
- ¼ teaspoon salt
- 1 cup granulated sugar
- ½ cup (1 stick) butter or margarine, softened
- 2 eggs
- 3 envelopes (1 ounce each) NESTLÉ® TOLL HOUSE® CHOCO BAKE® Unsweetened Chocolate Flavor
- 1 teaspoon vanilla extract
- ½ cup chopped nuts

FUDGE FROSTING:

- 3 tablespoons butter or margarine
- 1 envelope (1 ounce) NESTLÉ® TOLL HOUSE® CHOCO BAKE® Unsweetened Chocolate Flavor
- 2 teaspoons milk
- ½ teaspoon vanilla extract
- 1 cup sifted powdered sugar

For Brownies:

COMBINE flour, baking powder and salt in small bowl. Beat sugar, butter, eggs, Choco Bake and vanilla extract in small mixer bowl until creamy. Gradually beat in flour mixture. Stir in nuts. Spread into greased 8-inch square baking pan.

BAKE in preheated 350°F. oven for 25 to 30 minutes or until wooden pick inserted in center comes out slightly sticky. Cool brownies completely in pan on wire rack.

For Fudge Frosting:

BEAT butter, Choco Bake, milk and vanilla extract in small mixer bowl until well blended. Gradually beat in powdered sugar until creamy. Spread onto brownies. Cut into bars. Makes 16 brownies.

Double Espresso Brownies

ESPRESSO BROWNIES:
- 1 cup all-purpose flour
- ½ teaspoon baking powder
- ¼ teaspoon salt
- ⅓ cup hot water
- 1 tablespoon instant espresso powder or instant coffee crystals
- 1 cup granulated sugar
- ½ cup (1 stick) butter or margarine
- 2 cups (12-ounce package) NESTLÉ® TOLL HOUSE® Semi-Sweet Chocolate Morsels, *divided*
- 3 eggs

ESPRESSO FROSTING:
- ½ cup heavy whipping cream
- 1 teaspoon instant espresso powder or instant coffee crystals
- ½ cup sifted powdered sugar

For Espresso Brownies:

COMBINE flour, baking powder and salt in small bowl. Heat water and espresso in medium saucepan over low heat, stirring to dissolve powder. Add granulated sugar and butter; cook, stirring constantly, until mixture comes to a boil. Remove from heat; stir in 1 cup morsels until smooth. Add eggs, one at a time, stirring well after each addition. Stir in flour mixture. Pour into greased 9-inch square baking pan.

BAKE in preheated 350°F. oven for 25 to 30 minutes or until wooden pick inserted in center comes out slightly sticky. Cool completely in pan on wire rack.

For Espresso Frosting:

HEAT cream and espresso in small, heavy-duty saucepan over low heat, stirring to dissolve espresso. Add remaining morsels, stirring until smooth. Remove from heat; stir in powdered sugar. Refrigerate until frosting is of spreading consistency. Spread onto brownies. Cut into squares. Makes about 3 dozen brownies.

Double Chocolate Chip Brownies

2 cups (12-ounce package) NESTLÉ® TOLL HOUSE®
  Semi-Sweet Chocolate Morsels, *divided*
1 cup granulated sugar
½ cup unsweetened applesauce
2 tablespoons margarine
3 egg whites
1¼ cups all-purpose flour
¼ teaspoon baking soda
¼ teaspoon salt
1 teaspoon vanilla extract
¼ cup chopped nuts (optional)

HEAT 1 cup morsels, sugar, applesauce and margarine in large, heavy-duty saucepan over low heat; stir until smooth. Remove from heat. Cool slightly. Stir in egg whites. Combine flour, baking soda and salt. Stir into chocolate mixture. Stir in vanilla extract. Stir in remaining morsels and, if desired, nuts. Spread into greased 13 x 9-inch baking pan.

BAKE in preheated 350°F. oven for 16 to 20 minutes or just until set. Cool completely in pan on wire rack. Cut into bars. Makes about 2 dozen brownies.

Pictured on page 27.

White Chip Brownies

1 cup all-purpose flour
½ cup NESTLÉ® TOLL HOUSE® BAKING COCOA
¾ teaspoon baking powder
¼ teaspoon salt
1¼ cups granulated sugar
¾ cup (1½ sticks) butter or margarine, melted
2 teaspoons vanilla extract
3 eggs
2 cups (12-ounce package) NESTLÉ® TOLL HOUSE® Premier White Morsels, *divided*

COMBINE flour, cocoa, baking powder and salt in medium bowl. Beat granulated sugar, butter and vanilla extract together in large mixer bowl until creamy. Add eggs, one at a time, beating well after each addition. Gradually beat in flour mixture. Stir in 1½ cups morsels. Pour into greased 9-inch square baking pan.

BAKE in preheated 350° oven for 25 to 30 minutes or until wooden pick inserted in center comes out slightly sticky. Cool completely (center will sink) in pan on wire rack.

PLACE remaining morsels in small heavy-duty plastic bag. Microwave on MEDIUM-HIGH (70%) power for 45 seconds; knead bag to mix. Microwave at additional 10- to 20-second intervals, kneading until smooth. Cut a small hole in corner of bag; squeeze to drizzle over brownies. Refrigerate for 5 minutes or until drizzle is firm. Cut into bars. Makes 16 brownies.

Marbled Chocolate Brownies

1 ⅓ cups all-purpose flour
⅓ cup NESTLÉ® TOLL HOUSE® Baking Cocoa
¼ teaspoon baking soda
¼ teaspoon salt
1 ¼ cups granulated sugar
1 cup (6 ounces) NESTLÉ® TOLL HOUSE® Semi-Sweet
    Chocolate Morsels
½ cup unsweetened applesauce
2 tablespoons margarine
3 egg whites
1 teaspoon vanilla extract
4 ounces light cream cheese (Neufchâtel), softened
1 tablespoon granulated sugar
1 tablespoon nonfat milk

COMBINE flour, cocoa, baking soda and salt in small bowl. Heat 1 ¼ cups sugar, morsels, applesauce and margarine in a large, heavy-duty saucepan over low heat, stirring constantly just until morsels are melted. Remove from heat. Cool slightly. Stir in egg whites. Add flour mixture and vanilla extract; stir well. Spread into greased 13 x 9-inch baking pan.

STIR together cream cheese, 1 tablespoon sugar and milk in small bowl. Drop by rounded teaspoon over batter; swirl over surface of batter with back of spoon.

BAKE in preheated 325°F oven for 22 to 28 minutes or just until set. Cool completely in pan on wire rack. Cut into bars. Makes about 2 ½ dozen brownies.

Black Forest Brownie Squares

2 cups (12-ounce package) NESTLÉ® TOLL HOUSE®
  Semi-Sweet Chocolate Morsels, *divided*

½ cup butter or margarine, cut into pieces

3 eggs

1¼ cups all-purpose flour

1 cup granulated sugar

1 teaspoon vanilla extract

¼ teaspoon baking soda

1½ cups frozen whipped topping, thawed

2 cups (21-ounce can) cherry pie filling or topping

MELT 1 cup morsels and butter in large, heavy-duty saucepan over lowest possible heat, stirring until smooth. Remove from heat; stir in eggs. Gradually stir in flour, sugar, vanilla extract and baking soda. Stir in remaining morsels. Spread into greased 13 x 9-inch baking pan.

BAKE in preheated 350°F. oven for 20 to 25 minutes or until wooden pick inserted in center comes out slightly sticky. Cool completely in pan on wire rack. Spread with whipped topping. Top with pie filling. Cut into squares. Makes about 2 dozen squares.

Blonde Brownies

2¼ cups all-purpose flour
2½ teaspoons baking powder
½ teaspoon salt
1¾ cups packed brown sugar
¾ cups (1½ sticks) butter or margarine, softened
1 teaspoon vanilla extract
3 eggs
2 cups (12-ounce package) NESTLÉ® TOLL HOUSE®
Semi-Sweet Chocolate Morsels

COMBINE flour, baking powder and salt in small bowl. Beat brown sugar, butter and vanilla extract in large mixer bowl until creamy. Add eggs, one at a time, beating well after each addition. Gradually beat in flour mixture. Stir in morsels. Spread into greased 15 x 10-inch jelly-roll pan.

BAKE in preheated 350°F. oven for 20 to 25 minutes or until top is golden brown. Cool completely in pan on wire rack. Cut into bars Makes about 3 dozen brownies..

special occasion desserts

dazzle dinner guests with these showstopping desserts. Memorable meals rise to stellar heights when crowned with creamy Cappuccino Cheesecake, velvety Cream Cheese Flan or chocolate-drizzled Fruit-Filled Chocolate Chip Meringue Nests. For casual get-togethers, dish up Mocha Bread Pudding with Caramel Sauce. Turn the page and you're bound to find the perfect sweet ending to any black-tie dinner or family gathering.

Chocolate Chip Cheesecake (see recipe, page 85)

Marbled Pumpkin Cheesecake

CRUST:

1¼ cups graham cracker crumbs

¼ cup (½ stick) butter or margarine, melted

2 tablespoons granulated sugar

1 cup (6 ounces) NESTLÉ® TOLL HOUSE® Semi-Sweet Chocolate Mini Morsels, *divided*

FILLING:

3 packages (8 ounces each) cream cheese, softened

1 cup granulated sugar

¼ cup packed brown sugar

1¾ cups (15-ounce can) LIBBY'S® 100% Pure Pumpkin

4 eggs

½ cup NESTLÉ® CARNATION® Evaporated Milk

2 tablespoons cornstarch

1 teaspoon ground cinnamon

⅛ teaspoon ground nutmeg

For Crust:

COMBINE graham cracker crumbs, butter and granulated sugar in medium bowl. Press into bottom of greased 9-inch springform pan. Sprinkle with ½ cup morsels.

For Filling:

MICROWAVE remaining morsels in medium, microwave-safe bowl on HIGH (100%) power for 30 seconds; stir. Microwave at additional 10- to 20-second intervals, stirring until smooth; cool to room temperature.

BEAT cream cheese, granulated sugar and brown sugar in large mixer bowl until smooth; beat in pumpkin. Beat in eggs, evaporated milk, cornstarch, cinnamon and nutmeg. Remove ¾ cup pumpkin mixture; stir into melted chocolate. Pour remaining pumpkin mixture into crust. Spoon chocolate-pumpkin mixture over top; swirl with a knife.

BAKE in preheated 350°F. oven for 60 to 65 minutes or until edge is set but center still moves slightly. Cool in pan on wire rack. Refrigerate for several hours or overnight. Remove side of pan. Makes 12 to 16 servings.

Pictured on page 13.

Chocolate Chip Cheesecake

CRUST:

1½ cups (about 15) crushed chocolate sandwich cookies

2 tablespoons butter or margarine, melted

2 cups (12-ounce package) NESTLÉ® TOLL HOUSE® Semi-Sweet Chocolate Mini Morsels, *divided*

FILLING:

2 packages (8 ounces each) cream cheese, softened

½ cup granulated sugar

1 tablespoon vanilla extract

2 eggs

2 tablespoons all-purpose flour

¾ cup NESTLÉ® CARNATION® Evaporated Milk

½ cup sour cream

For Crust:
COMBINE crumbs with butter in medium bowl until moistened; press into bottom of ungreased 9-inch springform pan. Sprinkle with 1 cup morsels.

For Filling:
BEAT cream cheese, sugar and vanilla extract in large mixer bowl until smooth. Beat in eggs and flour. Gradually beat in evaporated milk and sour cream. Pour over crust. Sprinkle with remaining morsels.

BAKE in preheated 350°F. oven for 25 minutes. Cover loosely with aluminum foil. Bake for additional 30 to 40 minutes or until edge is set but center still moves slightly. Place in refrigerator immediately; refrigerate for 2 hours or until firm. Remove side of pan. Makes 12 to 16 servings.

NOTE: Cheesecake may be baked in 13 x 9-inch baking pan. Prepare as directed. Bake in preheated 300°F. oven for 20 minutes. Cover loosely with aluminum foil. Bake for additional 20 to 30 minutes.

Pictured on page 83.

Toffee Cheesecake

CRUST:

1¾ cups finely crushed toffee shortbread cookies (14 to 16 cookies)

4 teaspoons butter or margarine, melted

CHEESECAKE:

3 packages (8 ounces each) cream cheese, softened

1¼ cups packed brown sugar

1¾ cups (15-ounce can) LIBBY'S® 100% Pure Pumpkin

2 eggs

⅔ cup NESTLÉ® CARNATION® Evaporated Milk

2 tablespoons cornstarch

½ teaspoon ground cinnamon

⅔ cup chopped or crushed toffee candies (about 24 candies), *divided*

TOPPING:

2 cups (16-ounce carton) sour cream, at room temperature

¼ cup granulated sugar

½ teaspoon vanilla extract

Caramel-flavored ice cream topping (optional)

For Crust:

COMBINE crushed cookies and butter in small bowl. Press into bottom and 1 inch up side of 9-inch springform pan. Bake in preheated 350°F. oven for 6 to 8 minutes. Do not allow to brown. Cool on wire rack.

For Cheesecake:

BEAT cream cheese and brown sugar in large mixer bowl on medium speed until creamy. Beat in pumpkin, eggs, evaporated milk, cornstarch and cinnamon. Stir in ⅓ cup toffee pieces. Pour into prepared crust.

BAKE at 350°F. for 60 to 65 minutes or until edge is set but center still moves slightly.

For Topping:

COMBINE sour cream, granulated sugar, vanilla extract and remaining toffee pieces in small bowl. Spread over surface of warm cheesecake. Bake at 350°F. for 8 minutes more. Cool in pan on wire rack. Refrigerate several hours or overnight; remove side of pan. Before serving, drizzle with caramel topping, if desired. Makes 12 to 16 servings.

Maple Cheesecake

    ¾ cup graham cracker crumbs
    2 tablespoons margarine or butter, melted
    1¾ cups (15-ounce can) LIBBY'S® 100% Pure Pumpkin
    2 packages (8 ounces each) light cream cheese (Neufchâtel)
    1 cup packed brown sugar
    ½ cup part-skim-milk ricotta cheese
    2 tablespoons all-purpose flour
    1½ teaspoons pumpkin pie spice
    1½ teaspoons maple flavoring
    ½ cup NESTLÉ® CARNATION® Evaporated Fat Free Milk or
        Evaporated Lowfat Milk
    ½ cup egg substitute
        Maple Topping (recipe follows)
        Chopped pecans (optional)

COMBINE crumbs and margarine in small bowl. Press into bottom of 9-inch springform pan.

BEAT pumpkin, cream cheese, brown sugar, ricotta cheese, flour, pumpkin pie spice and maple flavoring in large mixer bowl on high speed for 1 minute. Beat in evaporated fat free milk and egg substitute just until blended. Pour over crust.

BAKE in preheated 350°F. oven for 65 to 85 minutes or until knife inserted halfway between center and outer edge comes out clean. Remove from oven; cool in pan on wire rack for 10 minutes. Spread with Maple Topping; refrigerate. To serve, remove side of pan and, if desired, sprinkle with pecans. Makes 16 servings.

For Maple Topping:
COMBINE ½ cup nonfat sour cream, 1 tablespoon granulated sugar and ¼ teaspoon maple flavoring in small bowl.

Pumpkin Cheesecake

CRUST:
- 1½ cups graham cracker crumbs
- ⅓ cup butter or margarine, melted
- ¼ cup granulated sugar

CHEESECAKE:
- 3 packages (8 ounces each) cream cheese, softened
- 1 cup granulated sugar
- ¼ cup packed brown sugar
- 1¾ cups (15-ounce can) LIBBY'S® 100% Pure Pumpkin
- 2 eggs
- 1 can (5 fluid ounces) NESTLÉ® CARNATION® Evaporated Milk
- 2 tablespoons cornstarch
- 1¼ teaspoons ground cinnamon
- ½ teaspoon ground nutmeg

TOPPING:
- 2 cups (16-ounce carton) sour cream, at room temperature
- ¼ to ⅓ cup granulated sugar
- 1 teaspoon vanilla extract
- Whole strawberries, sliced and fanned (optional)

For Crust:
COMBINE graham cracker crumbs, butter and sugar in medium bowl. Press into bottom and 1 inch up side of 9-inch springform pan. Bake in preheated 350°F. oven for 6 to 8 minutes. Do not allow to brown. Cool on wire rack.

For Cheesecake:
BEAT cream cheese, granulated sugar and brown sugar in large mixer bowl until fluffy. Beat in pumpkin, eggs and evaporated milk. Add cornstarch, cinnamon and nutmeg; beat well. Pour into crust.

BAKE at 350°F. for 55 to 60 minutes or until edge is set but center still moves slightly.

For Topping:
COMBINE sour cream, sugar and vanilla extract in small bowl. Spread over surface of warm cheesecake. Bake at 350°F. for 8 minutes more. Cool in pan on wire rack. Refrigerate for several hours or overnight; remove side of pan. If desired, garnish with strawberries. Makes 12 to 16 servings.

Pumpkin Orange Cheesecake

CRUST:
- ¾ cup graham cracker crumbs
- 2 tablespoons margarine or butter, melted

FILLING:
- 2 packages (8 ounces each) light cream cheese (Neufchâtel), softened
- ¾ cup packed brown sugar
- ½ cup nonfat ricotta cheese
- 1½ cups LIBBY'S® 100% Pure Pumpkin
- 3 tablespoons orange juice
- 2 tablespoons NESTLÉ® CARNATION® Evaporated Fat Free Milk
- 2 teaspoons vanilla extract
- 1½ teaspoons pumpkin pie spice
- 1 teaspoon grated orange peel
- ¾ cup frozen egg substitute, thawed
- Orange Topping (recipe follows)

For Crust:
COMBINE graham cracker crumbs and margarine in small bowl. Press into bottom of 9-inch springform pan.

For Filling:
BEAT cream cheese, brown sugar and ricotta cheese in large mixer bowl until fluffy. Add pumpkin, orange juice, evaporated fat free milk, vanilla extract, pumpkin pie spice and orange peel; beat until well blended. Add egg substitute and beat just until blended. Pour into prepared crust.

BAKE in preheated 350°F. oven for 60 to 65 minutes or until edge is set but center still moves slightly. Cool in pan on wire rack; spread with Orange Topping. Refrigerate several hours or overnight; remove side of pan. Makes 12 servings.

For Orange Topping:
COMBINE ½ cup light sour cream, 1 tablespoon granulated sugar and 1 teaspoon orange juice.

Cappuccino Cheesecake

1¾ cups (about 18) crushed chocolate cookies
½ cup granulated sugar, divided
⅓ cup butter, melted
3 packages (8 ounces each) cream cheese, softened
1 cup French Vanilla NESTLÉ® COFFEE-MATE® Liquid Creamer
4 eggs
6 teaspoons instant coffee crystals
¼ cup all-purpose flour
¾ cup NESTLÉ® TOLL HOUSE® Premier White Morsels
2 cups (16 ounce container) sour cream, at room temperature

COMBINE cookie crumbs and ¼ cup sugar in small bowl; stir in butter. Press onto bottom and 1 inch up side of ungreased 9-inch springform pan. Bake in preheated 350°F. oven for 5 minutes.

BEAT cream cheese and Coffee-Mate in large mixer bowl until creamy. Stir together eggs and coffee in medium bowl until coffee is dissolved. Add egg mixture, flour and remaining sugar to cream cheese mixture; beat until combined. Pour into chocolate crust.

BAKE at 350°F. for 45 to 50 minutes or until edge is set but center moves slightly.

MICROWAVE morsels in medium, microwave-safe bowl on MEDIUM-HIGH (70%) power for 1 minute; stir. Microwave at additional 10- to 20-second intervals, stirring until smooth. Stir in sour cream. Spread over top of cheesecake. Bake for additional 10 minutes. Cool in pan on wire rack. Refrigerate for several hours or overnight; remove side of pan. Makes 12 servings.

Tuxedo Cheesecake

CRUST:

1¾ cups (about 18) crushed chocolate sandwich cookies

2 tablespoons butter or margarine, melted

FILLING:

1 cup (6 ounces) NESTLÉ® TOLL HOUSE® Premier White Morsels

3 packages (8 ounces each) cream cheese, softened

¾ cup granulated sugar

2 teaspoons vanilla extract

3 eggs

1 bar (2 ounces) NESTLÉ® TOLL HOUSE® Semi-Sweet or Premier White Baking Bar, made into curls* or grated

For Crust:

TOSS cookie crumbs and butter together in medium bowl. Press into bottom of ungreased 9-inch springform pan. Bake in preheated 350°F. oven for 10 minutes.

For Filling:

MICROWAVE morsels in small, microwave-safe bowl on MEDIUM-HIGH (70%) power for 1 minute; stir. Microwave at additional 10- to 20-second intervals, stirring until smooth; cool to room temperature.

BEAT cream cheese, sugar and vanilla extract in large mixer bowl until smooth. Beat in eggs. Gradually beat in melted white morsels. Spread over chocolate crust.

BAKE at 350°F. for 40 to 50 minutes or until edge is set but center still moves slightly. Cool in pan on wire rack; refrigerate until firm. Remove side of pan. Garnish with chocolate curls* before serving. Makes 12 to 16 servings.

*NOTE: To make curls, carefully draw a vegetable peeler across a NESTLÉ® TOLL HOUSE® Semi-Sweet Chocolate or Premier White Baking Bar. Vary the width of your curls by using different sides of the chocolate bar.

Chocolate Intensity

CAKE:
- 4 bars (8-ounce box) NESTLÉ® TOLL HOUSE® Unsweetened Chocolate Baking Bars, broken into pieces
- 1½ cups granulated sugar
- ½ cup (1 stick) butter, softened
- 3 eggs
- 2 teaspoons vanilla extract
- ⅔ cup all-purpose flour

Sifted powdered sugar (optional)

COFFEE CRÈME SAUCE:
- 4 egg yolks, lightly beaten
- ⅓ cup granulated sugar
- 1 tablespoon instant coffee crystals
- 1½ cups milk
- 1 teaspoon vanilla extract

For Cake:

MICROWAVE baking bars in medium, microwave-safe bowl on HIGH (100%) power for 1 minute; stir. Microwave at additional 10- to 20-second intervals, stirring until smooth; cool to lukewarm.

BEAT sugar, butter, eggs and vanilla extract in small mixer bowl for about 4 minutes or until thick and pale yellow. Beat in melted chocolate. Gradually beat in flour. Spread into greased 9-inch springform pan.

BAKE in preheated 350°F. oven for 25 to 28 minutes or until wooden pick inserted in center comes out moist. Cool in pan on wire rack for 15 minutes. Loosen and remove side of pan; cool completely. Sprinkle, if desired, with powdered sugar; serve with Coffee Crème Sauce. Makes 12 servings.

For Coffee Crème Sauce:

PLACE egg yolks in medium bowl. Combine sugar and coffee crystals in medium saucepan; stir in milk. Cook over medium heat, stirring constantly, until mixture comes just to a simmer. Remove from heat. Gradually whisk half of hot milk mixture into egg yolks; return mixture to saucepan. Cook, stirring constantly, for 3 to 4 minutes or until mixture is slightly thickened. Strain into small bowl; stir in vanilla extract. Cover; refrigerate.

Individual Chocolate Espresso Soufflés

Nonstick cooking spray
2 tablespoons granulated sugar
½ cup NESTLÉ® TOLL HOUSE® Baking Cocoa
½ cup hot water
3 tablespoons instant espresso powder or instant coffee crystals
2 tablespoons butter
3 tablespoons all-purpose flour
¾ cup NESTLÉ® CARNATION® Evaporated Milk
¾ cup granulated sugar, *divided*
4 egg whites
Pinch of salt
Sifted powdered sugar

SPRAY eight 6-ounce custard cups with nonstick cooking spray; sprinkle evenly with 2 tablespoons granulated sugar.

COMBINE cocoa, water and espresso powder in medium bowl; stir until smooth. Melt butter in small saucepan over medium heat. Stir in flour; cook, stirring constantly, for 1 minute. Stir in evaporated milk and ½ cup granulated sugar. Cook, whisking frequently, for 2 to 3 minutes or until mixture is slightly thickened. Remove from heat. Add to cocoa mixture; stir until smooth.

BEAT egg whites and pinch of salt in small mixer bowl until soft peaks form. Gradually beat in remaining sugar until stiff peaks form. Fold one-fourth of egg whites into chocolate mixture to lighten. Fold in remaining egg whites gently but thoroughly. Pour mixture into prepared cups, filling ¾ full. Place on baking sheet.

BAKE in preheated 375°F. oven 18 to 20 minutes or until wooden pick inserted in center comes out moist but not wet. Sprinkle with powdered sugar. Serve immediately. Makes 8 servings.

Fruit-Filled Chocolate Chip Meringue Nests

MERINGUES:

- 4 egg whites
- ½ teaspoon salt
- ½ teaspoon cream of tartar
- 1 cup granulated sugar
- 2 cups (12-ounce package) NESTLÉ® TOLL HOUSE® Semi-Sweet Chocolate Morsels

CHOCOLATE SAUCE:

- 1 can (5 ounces) NESTLÉ® CARNATION® Evaporated Milk
- 1 cup (6 ounces) NESTLÉ® TOLL HOUSE® Semi-Sweet Chocolate Morsels
- 1 tablespoon granulated sugar
- 1 teaspoon vanilla extract Dash salt
- 3 cups fresh berries or fruit (whole blueberries, raspberries or blackberries and/or chopped kiwi, peaches or strawberries)

For Meringues:

BEAT egg whites, salt and cream of tartar in large mixer bowl until soft peaks form. Gradually add sugar, a tablespoon at a time, beating about 7 minutes, until stiff peaks form and sugar is dissolved. Gently fold in morsels. Spread meringue into ten 3-inch nests with deep wells about 2 inches apart on lightly greased baking sheets.

BAKE in preheated 300°F. oven for 35 to 45 minutes or until meringues are dry and crisp. Cool on baking sheets for 5 minutes; remove to wire racks to cool completely.

For Chocolate Sauce:

HEAT evaporated milk to boiling in small, heavy-duty saucepan. Stir in morsels. Cook, stirring constantly, until mixture is slightly thickened and smooth. Remove from heat; stir in sugar, vanilla extract and salt.

FILL meringues with fruit and drizzle with Chocolate Sauce; serve immediately. Makes 10 servings.

special occasion desserts

Chocolate Rhapsody

CAKE LAYER:
- ⅔ cup all-purpose flour
- ½ teaspoon baking powder
- ¼ teaspoon salt
- 6 tablespoons butter or margarine, softened
- ½ cup granulated sugar
- 1 egg
- 1 teaspoon vanilla extract
- ¼ cup milk

CHOCOLATE LAYER:
- 2 cups (12-ounce package) NESTLÉ® TOLL HOUSE® Semi-Sweet Chocolate Morsels
- ¾ cup heavy whipping cream

RASPBERRY MOUSSE:
- ⅓ cup granulated sugar
- 2 tablespoons water
- 1 teaspoon cornstarch
- 2 cups (8 ounces) slightly sweetened or unsweetened frozen raspberries, thawed
- 3 bars (6-ounce box) NESTLÉ® TOLL HOUSE® Premier White Baking Bars, broken into pieces
- 1¾ cups heavy whipping cream, *divided*
- 1 teaspoon vanilla extract
  Fresh raspberries (optional)

For Cake Layer:
COMBINE flour, baking powder and salt in small bowl. Beat butter and sugar in small mixer bowl until creamy. Beat in egg and vanilla extract. Alternately beat in flour mixture and milk. Spread into greased 9-inch springform pan.

BAKE in preheated 350°F. oven for 15 to 20 minutes or until lightly browned. Cool completely in pan on wire rack.

For Chocolate Layer:
MICROWAVE morsels and cream in medium, microwave-safe bowl on HIGH (100%) power for 1 minute; stir. Microwave at additional 10- to 20-second intervals, stirring until smooth. Cool completely.

For Raspberry Mousse:
COMBINE sugar, water and cornstarch in medium saucepan; stir in raspberries Bring mixture to a boil. Boil, stirring constantly, for 1 minute. Cool completely.

MICROWAVE baking bars and ½ cup cream in medium, microwave-safe bowl on MEDIUM-HIGH (70%) power for 1 minute; stir. Microwave at additional 10- to 20-second intervals, stirring until smooth. Cool completely. Stir into raspberry mixture.

BEAT remaining cream and vanilla extract in large mixer bowl until stiff peaks form. Fold in raspberry mixture.

To Assemble:

REMOVE side of springform pan; dust off crumbs. Grease inside of pan; reattach side. Spread ½ cup chocolate mixture over cake layer; freeze for 5 minutes. Spoon raspberry mousse over chocolate; freeze for 10 minutes. Carefully spread remaining chocolate mixture over raspberry mousse. Refrigerate for at least 4 hours or until firm. Carefully remove side of springform pan. If desired, garnish with raspberries. Makes 12 servings.

Cream Cheese-Chocolate Chip Pastry Cookies

1 package (17¼ ounces) frozen puff pastry, thawed according to package directions (2 sheets)
1 package (8 ounces) cream cheese, softened
3 tablespoons granulated sugar
2 cups (11½-ounce package) NESTLÉ® TOLL HOUSE® Milk Chocolate Morsels, *divided*

ROLL 1 sheet puff pastry to 14 x 10-inch rectangle on floured surface. Combine cream cheese and granulated sugar in small bowl.

SPREAD half of cream cheese mixture over puff pastry, leaving 1-inch border on 1 long side. Sprinkle with 1 cup morsels. Roll up, starting at long side covered with cream cheese. Seal edge by dampening with water. Repeat with remaining ingredients. Refrigerate for 1 hour. Cut rolls crosswise into 1-inch-thick slices. Place cut side up on parchment paper-lined or lightly greased baking sheets.

BAKE in preheated 375°F. oven for 20 to 25 minutes or until golden brown. Let stand for 2 minutes; remove to wire racks to cool completely. Makes about 2 dozen cookies.

Mini Cream Cheese Flans

1 cup granulated sugar

½ cup water

1½ cups (12 fluid-ounce can) NESTLÉ® CARNATION® Evaporated Milk

1 can (14 ounces) NESTLÉ® CARNATION® Sweetened Condensed Milk

1 package (8 ounces) cream cheese, softened

¼ cup (½ stick) butter, softened

5 eggs

1 teaspoon vanilla extract

COMBINE sugar and water in small saucepan. Cook, stirring constantly, over low heat for 2 minutes or until sugar is dissolved. Bring to a boil. Boil, without stirring, for 10 to 15 minutes or until golden brown. Quickly pour evenly into twelve 10-ounce custard cups. Tip cups to coat bottoms and sides with sugar syrup.

COMBINE evaporated milk, sweetened condensed milk, cream cheese, butter, eggs and vanilla extract in blender container; cover. Blend until smooth. Pour into prepared cups.

FILL two 13x9-inch baking pans with hot water. Divide the filled cups between the baking pans.

BAKE in preheated 350°F. oven for 35 to 45 minutes or until knife inserted near center comes out clean. Cool in pans on wire racks for 20 minutes. Remove custard cups from baking pans; refrigerate for several hours or overnight. Run knife around rims; shake gently to loosen. Invert onto serving dishes. Makes 12 servings.

Vanilla Flan

¾ cup granulated sugar
1 can (12 fluid ounces) NESTLÉ® CARNATION® Evaporated Milk
1 can (14 ounces) NESTLÉ® CARNATION® Sweetened Condensed Milk
3 eggs
1 tablespoon vanilla extract

HEAT sugar in small, heavy-duty saucepan over medium-low heat, stirring constantly, for 3 to 4 minutes or until dissolved and caramel colored. Quickly pour onto bottom of deep-dish 9-inch pie plate; swirl around bottom and sides to coat.

COMBINE evaporated milk, sweetened condensed milk, eggs and vanilla extract in medium bowl. Pour into prepared pie plate. Place pie plate in large roasting pan; fill roasting pan with warm water to about 1-inch depth.

BAKE in preheated 325°F. oven for 45 to 50 minutes or until knife inserted near center comes out clean. Remove flan from water. Cool on wire rack. Refrigerate for 4 hours or overnight.

TO SERVE, run small spatula around edge of pie plate. Invert serving plate over pie plate. Turn over; shake gently to release. Caramelized sugar forms sauce. Makes 8 servings.

Flan Hints

If you're tempted to skip the hot water bath when baking a flan, don't. The hot water helps keep the heat even so the flan cooks slowly without overcooking on the edges.

When testing to see if a flan is done, insert a clean knife ½ inch into the flan just off center. If the knife comes out clean, the flan is done. If any of the flan clings to the knife, bake a few more minutes and test again.

Once the flan tests done, remove it from the water immediately. If it stays in the hot water, it will continue to cook.

Cream Cheese Flans

¾ cup granulated sugar
1 can (12 fluid ounces) NESTLÉ® CARNATION® Evaporated Milk
1 can (14 ounces) NESTLÉ® CARNATION® Sweetened Condensed Milk
1 package (8 ounces) cream cheese, softened, cut into chunks
5 eggs

PLACE sugar in small, heavy-duty saucepan. Cook over medium-high heat, stirring constantly, for 3 to 4 minutes or until sugar is dissolved and golden. Quickly pour into eight 10-ounce custard cups;* tip cups to coat bottoms and sides with sugar syrup.

PLACE evaporated milk, sweetened condensed milk and cream cheese in food processor or blender container; cover. Process until smooth. Add eggs; process until well mixed. Pour mixture into prepared cups. Place cups in 2 large baking pans; fill pans with hot water to 1-inch depth.

BAKE in preheated 350°F. oven for 30 to 40 minutes or until knife inserted near centers comes out clean. Remove cups from water; cool cups on wire racks for 30 minutes; refrigerate for several hours or overnight. To serve, run small spatula around edges of cups; gently shake flans to loosen. Invert onto serving dishes to serve. Makes 8 servings.

*NOTE: To make one large flan, use one 2-quart casserole dish instead of custard cups. Coat with melted sugar syrup and pour milk mixture into dish as above. Place dish in large baking pan; fill pan halfway with hot water. Bake in preheated 350°F. oven for 60 to 70 minutes or until knife inserted in center comes out clean. Cool. Refrigerate; invert as above onto a serving platter. Slice into wedges.

Pumpkin Caramel Flan

¾ cup granulated sugar

4 eggs

1 cup LIBBY'S® 100% Pure Pumpkin

⅓ cup honey

1 to 1½ teaspoons pumpkin pie spice

1 teaspoon vanilla extract

½ teaspoon salt

1 can (12 fluid ounces) NESTLÉ® CARNATION®
   Evaporated Milk

Nasturtium blossoms (optional)

PLACE 8-inch square baking dish into 13 x 9-inch baking dish; fill outer dish with hot water to ¾-inch depth.

HEAT sugar in heavy skillet over medium heat, stirring constantly, until melted and golden brown; pour into square dish. Remove square dish from water; working quickly, swirl melted sugar around bottom and sides of dish to coat. Return dish to water.

COMBINE eggs, pumpkin, honey, pumpkin pie spice, vanilla extract and salt in medium bowl. Add evaporated milk; mix well. Pour into prepared square baking dish.

BAKE in preheated 350°F. oven for 40 to 45 minutes or until knife inserted near center comes out clean. Remove square baking dish from water; cool on wire rack. Cover and refrigerate for 4 hours or overnight. To serve, run small spatula around edge of dish. Invert serving plate over baking dish. Invert baking dish; shake gently to release. Cut flan diagonally into quarters; cut each quarter in half to form triangles. Spoon some of the caramel syrup from baking dish over each serving. Garnish with edible nasturtium blossoms, if desired. Makes 8 servings.

For Lower-Fat Flan:
USE 2 eggs and 2 egg whites in place of the 4 eggs and NESTLÉ® CARNATION® Evaporated Fat Free Milk in place of the evaporated milk. Prepare and bake as above. Makes 8 servings.

Pumpkin Pear Strudel

2 small pears, peeled, cored and diced (about 2 cups)

1 cup LIBBY'S® 100% Pure Pumpkin

¾ cup packed brown sugar

¾ cup chopped walnuts

1 teaspoon ground cinnamon

⅛ teaspoon ground cloves

⅛ teaspoon ground ginger

1 package (17¼ ounces) frozen puff pastry, thawed according to package directions (2 sheets)

1 egg, lightly beaten

Cinnamon Sugar (recipe follows)

MIX pears, pumpkin, brown sugar, walnuts, cinnamon, cloves and ginger in medium bowl. Spoon half of the pear mixture down the center ⅓ of 1 pastry sheet. Make downward slanting cuts in outer edges of pastry about ¾ inch apart, cutting from outside edges to within about 1 inch of pear mixture. Starting at top, fold side pastry strips alternately over filling, forming chevron design (see photo, left). Seal top and bottom ends of strudel. Place on rimmed baking sheet. Repeat with remaining pear mixture and remaining pastry sheet. Brush both strudels with egg; sprinkle with Cinnamon Sugar.

BAKE in preheated 375°F. oven for 25 to 30 minutes or until golden brown and puffy. Cool slightly on baking sheet on wire rack. Serve warm or at room temperature. Makes 10 servings.

For Cinnamon Sugar:
COMBINE ¼ cup granulated sugar and ¾ teaspoon ground cinnamon in small bowl.

Pumpkin Pecan Bread Pudding

  5 cups ¾-inch French bread cubes (about ½ of a
       1-pound loaf)
1¾ cups (15-ounce can) LIBBY'S® 100% Pure Pumpkin, *divided*
  1 can (12 fluid ounces) NESTLÉ® CARNATION®
       Evaporated Milk
  3 eggs
  ½ cup packed brown sugar
  ½ cup coarsely chopped pecans
  1 teaspoon vanilla extract
  ¾ teaspoon ground cinnamon
  ¼ teaspoon ground nutmeg
       Pumpkin Caramel Sauce (recipe follows)

PLACE bread in greased 8-inch square baking pan. Combine 1 cup
pumpkin, evaporated milk, eggs, brown sugar, pecans, vanilla
extract, cinnamon and nutmeg in medium bowl. Pour over bread;
press bread into egg mixture. Place square pan into 13 x 9-inch
baking pan; fill outer pan with hot water to 1-inch depth. Bake in
preheated 350°F. oven for 45 to 50 minutes or until set. Serve with
Pumpkin Caramel Sauce. Makes 6 servings.

For Pumpkin Caramel Sauce:
COMBINE ½ cup caramel- or butterscotch-flavored ice cream
topping, remaining pumpkin and ¼ teaspoon ground cinnamon in
medium saucepan. Warm over low heat, stirring frequently. Do not
allow mixture to boil.

Mocha Bread Pudding with Caramel Sauce

BREAD PUDDING:

- 9 cups 1-inch French bread cubes (about ¾ of a 1-pound loaf)
- 1 cup granulated sugar
- ¼ cup NESTLÉ® TOLL HOUSE® Baking Cocoa
- 1 tablespoon instant coffee crystals
- 4 eggs
- 2 cans (12 fluid ounces each) NESTLÉ® CARNATION® Evaporated Fat Free Milk or Evaporated Lowfat Milk, *divided*
- 2 teaspoons vanilla extract

CARAMEL SAUCE:

- ⅔ cup packed brown sugar
- ¼ cup (½ stick) butter or margarine
- 1 tablespoon light corn syrup

For Bread Pudding:

PLACE bread cubes in greased 2-quart baking dish. Combine sugar, cocoa and coffee granules in small bowl.

BEAT eggs, 2⅔ cups evaporated milk and vanilla extract in medium bowl until well blended; stir in sugar mixture. Pour over bread, pressing bread into milk mixture.

BAKE in preheated 350°F. oven for 50 to 55 minutes or until set.

For Caramel Sauce:

COMBINE brown sugar, butter and corn syrup in small saucepan. Cook over medium-low heat, stirring constantly, for 2 to 3 minutes or until sugar is dissolved. Slowly stir in remaining evaporated milk. Bring to a boil, stirring constantly; cook for 1 minute. Remove from heat. Serve with warm bread pudding. Makes 12 servings.

Melted Chocolate Magic

A touch of melted chocolate adds elegance to cookies, cakes, pies and candies, as well as many other desserts. Keep these decorating hints in mind the next time you want to dress up something sweet for your family or company. Start first by melting the chocolate (see Masterful Melting, page 234); use it to make one of these attractive trims.

Chocolate-Dipped Nuts: Dip large nuts halfway into melted chocolate; let excess chocolate drip off. For small nuts, use a small paintbrush to stroke on the chocolate. Place the nuts on waxed paper to dry.

Chocolate Leaves: Use nontoxic leaves, such as mint, lemon or strawberry leaves. With a small paint brush, apply two or three coats of melted chocolate to the underside of each leaf. Wipe off any chocolate on the topside of the leaf. Allow the chocolate to set up between coats. Place the leaves, chocolate sides up, on a waxed-paper-lined baking sheet; chill until hardened. Before using, peel the leaf away from the chocolate.

Chocolate Designs: Place slightly cooled, melted chocolate in a heavy-duty plastic bag. Cut a small hole in the corner of the bag. Drizzle heart shapes or other designs onto waxed paper. Refrigerate until firm.

Chocolate Cutouts: Melt 1 cup (6 ounces) of NESTLÉ® TOLL HOUSE® Semi-Sweet Chocolate Morsels or 1 cup (6 ounces) NESTLÉ® TOLL HOUSE® Premier White Morsels with 1 tablespoon shortening; cool slightly. Pour the chocolate mixture onto a waxed paper-lined baking sheet, spreading it $1/8$- to $1/4$-inch thick. Chill the chocolate until almost set. Firmly press hors d'oeuvre or small cookie cutters into the chocolate. Refrigerate. Before serving, lift the cutouts from the baking sheet.

Chocolate-Dipped Fruit: Melt 1 cup (6 ounces) of NESTLÉ® TOLL HOUSE® Semi-Sweet Chocolate Morsels or 1 cup (6 ounces) NESTLÉ® TOLL HOUSE® Premier White Morsels with 2 tablespoons shortening. Dip fruit into chocolate mixture; shake off excess. Place on waxed paper-lined baking sheet; refrigerate until firm.

Summer Berry Brownie Torte

¾ cup granulated sugar
6 tablespoons butter or margarine
1 tablespoon water
1½ cups (9 ounces) NESTLÉ® TOLL HOUSE® Semi-Sweet
  Chocolate Morsels, *divided*
½ teaspoon vanilla extract
2 eggs
⅔ cup all-purpose flour
¼ teaspoon baking soda
¼ teaspoon salt
  Filling (recipe follows)
2 cups sliced strawberries and/or blueberries

COMBINE sugar, butter and water in small, heavy-duty saucepan. Bring to a boil, stirring constantly; remove from heat. Add ¾ cup morsels; stir until smooth. Stir in vanilla extract. Add eggs, one at a time, stirring well after each addition. Add flour, baking soda and salt; stir until well blended. Stir in remaining morsels. Pour into waxed paper-lined and greased 9-inch round cake pan.

BAKE in preheated 350°F. oven for 20 to 25 minutes or until wooden pick inserted in center comes out slightly sticky. Cool in pan on wire rack for 15 minutes. Invert onto wire rack; remove waxed paper. Turn right side up; cool completely. Spread filling over brownie; top with berries. Refrigerate until serving time. Makes 8 to 10 servings.

For Filling:
BEAT ½ cup heavy whipping cream and ¼ cup granulated sugar in small mixer bowl until stiff peaks form.

kids' stuff

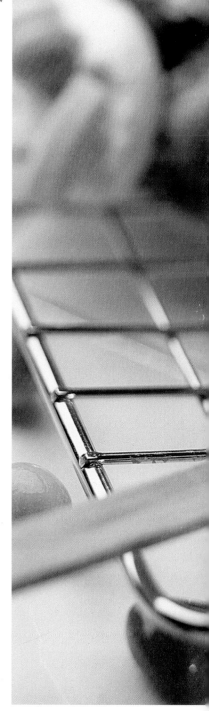

score big with the kids by whipping up one of these winning treats. For an after-school snack, set out a plate of Oatmeal Scotchies and a pitcher of ice-cold milk. Looking for a way to keep little hands busy? Let the kids decorate Monster Pops. Scary creatures are easy to create with these giant-size cookies baked on a stick. Turn the page and find the perfect cookie, candy or other sweet to delight the child in you life.

Monster Pops (see recipe, page 114)

Monster Pops

1⅔ cups all-purpose flour

1 teaspoon baking soda

½ teaspoon salt

1 cup (2 sticks) butter or margarine, softened

¾ cup granulated sugar

¾ cup packed brown sugar

2 teaspoons vanilla extract

2 eggs

2 cups (12-ounce package) NESTLÉ® TOLL HOUSE® Semi-Sweet Chocolate Morsels

2 cups quick or old-fashioned oats

1 cup raisins

About 24 wooden craft sticks

1 container (16 ounces) prepared vanilla frosting, colored as desired, or colored icing in tubes

Assorted colored candies

COMBINE flour, baking soda and salt in small bowl. Beat butter, granulated sugar, brown sugar and vanilla extract in large mixer bowl until creamy. Beat in eggs. Gradually beat in flour mixture. Stir in morsels, oats and raisins. Drop dough by level ¼-cup measure 3 inches apart onto ungreased baking sheets. Shape into round mounds. Insert wooden stick into side of each mound.

BAKE in preheated 325°F. oven for 14 to 18 minutes or until golden brown. Let stand for 2 minutes; remove to wire racks to cool completely.

DECORATE pops as desired. Makes about 2 dozen cookies.

For Speedy Monster Pops:
SUBSTITUTE 2 packages (18 ounces each) NESTLÉ® TOLL HOUSE® Refrigerated Chocolate Chip Cookie Dough for the first nine ingredients, adding 1 cup quick or old-fashioned oats and ½ cup raisins to the dough. Bake as directed for 16 to 20 minutes or until golden brown. Cool and decorate as desired. Makes about 1½ dozen cookies.

Pictured on pages 112-113.

Disappearing Chocolate Bars

1¼ cups granulated sugar
1 cup (2 sticks) plus 3 tablespoons butter or margarine, softened, *divided*
1 cup NESTLÉ® TOLL HOUSE® Baking Cocoa, *divided*
2 eggs
1 egg white
2½ teaspoons vanilla extract
½ teaspoon salt
1¼ cups all-purpose flour
⅔ cup plus ¼ cup NESTLÉ® CARNATION® Evaporated Milk, *divided*
1¼ cups chopped walnuts
1 cup sifted powdered sugar

COMBINE granulated sugar, 1 cup butter, ⅔ cup cocoa, eggs, egg white, vanilla extract and salt in large mixer bowl; beat until light and fluffy. Alternately beat in flour and ⅔ cup evaporated milk just until blended. Fold in walnuts. Spread into greased 13 x 9-inch baking pan.

BAKE in preheated 350°F. oven for 20 to 25 minutes or until wooden pick inserted in center comes out clean. Cool completely in pan on wire rack.

MELT remaining butter. Combine with remaining cocoa in medium bowl; stir well. Alternately stir in powdered sugar and remaining evaporated milk. Stir vigorously until smooth. Frost cooled cookies. Cut into bars. Makes about 2 dozen bars.

Great Pumpkin Cookies

 2 cups all-purpose flour
1⅓ cups quick or old-fashioned oats
 1 teaspoon baking soda
 1 teaspoon ground cinnamon
 ½ teaspoon salt
 1 cup (2 sticks) butter or margarine, softened
 1 cup granulated sugar
 1 cup packed brown sugar
 1 cup LIBBY'S® 100% Pure Pumpkin
 1 egg
 1 teaspoon vanilla extract
 ¾ cup chopped nuts
 ¾ cup raisins
   Colored icings in tubes
   NESTLÉ® TOLL HOUSE® Semi-Sweet Chocolate Morsels
   Assorted colored candies

COMBINE flour, oats, baking soda, cinnamon and salt in medium bowl. Beat butter, granulated sugar and brown sugar in large mixer bowl until creamy. Beat in pumpkin, egg and vanilla extract until well mixed. Gradually beat in flour mixture. Stir in nuts and raisins. For each cookie, drop about ¼ cup dough onto greased baking sheet; spread dough into round, triangular or oval shapes about 3 inches across.

BAKE in preheated 350°F. oven for 14 to 16 minutes or until cookies are firm and lightly browned. Let stand for 2 minutes; remove to wire racks to cool completely. Decorate with icing, morsels and assorted candies. Makes about 20 large cookies.

Butterscotch Haystacks

1⅔ cups (11-ounce package) NESTLÉ® TOLL HOUSE®
   Butterscotch Morsels

¾ cup creamy peanut butter

1 can (8.5 ounces total) or 2 cans (5 ounces each) chow
   mein noodles

3½ cups miniature marshmallows

LINE baking sheets or trays with waxed paper.

MICROWAVE morsels in large, microwave-safe bowl on
MEDIUM-HIGH (70%) power for 1 minute; stir. Microwave at
additional 10- to 20-second intervals, stirring until smooth. Stir in
peanut butter until well blended. Add chow mein noodles and
marshmallows; toss until coated. Drop by rounded tablespoon onto
prepared sheets. Refrigerate until ready to serve. Makes about
6 dozen candies.

Chocolate Cookie Turtle Shapes

2 cups (about 120 halves) pecan halves
1 package (18 ounces) refrigerated NESTLÉ® TOLL HOUSE®
   Chocolate Chip Cookie Dough
20 caramels, unwrapped
2 tablespoons milk

SOAK pecans in water for 5 minutes. To make one turtle cookie, arrange 5 pecans on ungreased baking sheet (1 for head, 4 for legs), leaving about a 1-inch circle in center.

SHAPE level tablespoon of cookie dough into ball; place over circle, pressing onto pecans. Repeat with remaining pecans and dough, placing turtles 2 inches apart on ungreased baking sheets.

BAKE in preheated 350°F. oven for 11 to 13 minutes or until edges are crisp. Let stand for 1 minute; remove to wire racks to cool completely.

MICROWAVE caramels and milk in microwave-safe bowl on HIGH (100%) power for 1½ minutes; stir. Microwave at additional 10-second intervals until melted. Drizzle over turtles. Makes about 2 dozen cookies.

Cookie Care Packages

When you plan to mail cookies, choose a recipe for firm cookies, avoiding soft, brittle or delicate varieties. Drop cookies, slice-and-bake cookies and uncut bar cookies travel best. Avoid frosted cookies because they may stick to each other or to the packaging. After baking, cool the cookies completely; wrap two at a time, back to back, in plastic wrap. Stack cookies snugly, on end, in a sturdy box, using a filler such as bubble wrap, foam packing pieces or crumpled waxed paper or paper towels to fill in extra spaces. Seal, label and mail.

Chocolate Gingerbread Boys and Girls

2 cups (12-ounce package) NESTLÉ® TOLL HOUSE® Semi-Sweet Chocolate Morsels, *divided*

2¾ cups all-purpose flour

1 teaspoon baking soda

½ teaspoon salt

½ teaspoon ground ginger

½ teaspoon ground cinnamon

3 tablespoons butter or margarine, softened

3 tablespoons granulated sugar

½ cup molasses

¼ cup water

Prepared vanilla frosting or colored icing in tubes

MICROWAVE 1½ cup morsels in medium, microwave-safe bowl on HIGH (100%) power for 1 minute; stir. Microwave at additional 10- to 20-second intervals, stirring until smooth. Cool to room temperature.

COMBINE flour, baking soda, salt, ginger and cinnamon in medium bowl. Beat butter and granulated sugar in small mixer bowl until creamy. Beat in molasses and melted chocolate. Gradually add flour mixture alternately with water, beating until smooth. Cover and chill for 1 hour or until firm.

ROLL half of dough to ¼-inch thickness on floured surface with floured rolling pin. Cut into gingerbread boys and girls, using cookie cutters or a stencil. Place on ungreased baking sheets. Repeat with remaining dough.

BAKE in preheated 350°F. oven for 5 to 6 minutes or until edges are set but centers are still slightly soft. Let stand for 2 minutes; remove to wire racks to cool completely

PLACE remaining morsels in small heavy-duty plastic bag. Microwave on HIGH (100%) power for 45 seconds; knead. Microwave at additional 10-second intervals, kneading until smooth. Cut a small hole in corner of bag; squeeze to pipe over cookies. Decorate with piped frosting or icing. Makes about 2½ dozen cookies.

Peanut Butter and Jelly Bars

1¼ cups all-purpose flour
½ cup graham cracker crumbs
½ teaspoon baking soda
½ teaspoon salt
½ cup (1 stick) butter, softened
½ cup granulated sugar
½ cup packed brown sugar
½ cup creamy peanut butter
1 egg
1 teaspoon vanilla extract
1¾ cups (11.5-ounce package) NESTLÉ® TOLL HOUSE® Milk Chocolate Morsels
¾ cup coarsely chopped peanuts
½ cup jelly or jam

COMBINE flour, graham cracker crumbs, baking soda and salt in small bowl.

BEAT butter, granulated sugar, brown sugar and peanut butter in large mixer bowl until creamy. Beat in egg and vanilla extract. Gradually beat in flour mixture. Stir in morsels and peanuts. Press ¾ of the dough into ungreased 13 x 9-inch baking pan.

BAKE in preheated 350°F. oven for 15 minutes; remove from oven. Drop jelly by heaping teaspoon over partially baked dough. Let stand for 1 minute; spread to cover. Drop remaining dough by heaping teaspoon over jelly. Bake for additional 20 to 25 minutes or until edges are set. Cool completely in pan on wire rack. Cut into bars. Makes about 4 dozen bars.

Milk Chocolate Oatmeal Cookies

1¼ cups all-purpose flour
½ teaspoon baking powder
½ teaspoon baking soda
½ teaspoon ground cinnamon
¼ teaspoon salt
¾ cup (1½ sticks) butter or margarine, softened
¾ cup packed brown sugar
⅓ cup granulated sugar
1½ teaspoons vanilla extract
1 egg
2 tablespoons milk
2 cups (11½-ounce package) NESTLÉ® TOLL HOUSE® Milk Chocolate Morsels
1 cup quick or old-fashioned oats
½ cup raisins (optional)

COMBINE flour, baking powder, baking soda, cinnamon and salt in small bowl. Beat butter, brown sugar, granulated sugar and vanilla extract in large mixer bowl until creamy. Beat in egg. Gradually beat in flour mixture and milk. Stir in morsels, oats and, if desired, raisins. Drop by tablespoon onto ungreased baking sheets.

BAKE in preheated 375°F. oven for 10 to 14 minutes or until edges are crisp but centers are still soft. Let stand for 2 minutes; remove to wire racks to cool completely. Makes about 3 dozen cookies.

Chocolate Peanut Cookies

2 bars (2 ounces each) NESTLÉ® TOLL HOUSE® Semi-Sweet Chocolate Baking Bars, broken into pieces
1¼ cups all-purpose flour
¾ teaspoon baking soda
½ teaspoon salt
½ cup (1 stick) butter or margarine, softened
½ cup packed brown sugar
¼ cup granulated sugar
2 teaspoons vanilla extract
1 egg
1½ cups coarsely chopped honey-roasted peanuts

MICROWAVE baking bars in small microwave-safe bowl on HIGH (100%) power for 1 minute; stir. Microwave at additional 10- to 20-second intervals, stirring until smooth; cool.

COMBINE flour, baking soda and salt in small bowl. Beat butter, brown sugar, granulated sugar and vanilla extract in large mixer bowl. Beat in melted chocolate and egg. Gradually beat in flour mixture. Stir in peanuts. Drop by rounded tablespoon onto ungreased baking sheets.

BAKE in preheated 375°F. oven for 8 to 9 minutes or until edges are set but centers are still slightly soft. Let stand for 3 minutes; remove to wire racks to cool completely. Makes about 2½ dozen cookies.

Giant Decorated Chocolate Chip Cookies

2 cups all-purpose flour
1 teaspoon baking soda
¼ teaspoon salt
1¼ cups packed brown sugar
1 cup (2 sticks) butter or margarine, softened
1 teaspoon vanilla extract
1 egg
2 cups (11½-ounce package) NESTLÉ® TOLL HOUSE® Milk Chocolate Morsels, *divided*
1 cup chopped nuts
1 cup raisins
2 containers (16 ounces each) prepared vanilla frosting
Colored icing in tubes
Assorted colored candies

COMBINE flour, baking soda and salt in small bowl. Beat brown sugar, butter and vanilla extract in large mixer bowl until creamy. Beat in egg. Gradually beat in flour mixture. Stir in 1½ cups morsels, nuts and raisins. Drop ½ cup dough onto ungreased baking sheets; spread to 4-inch circle. Repeat with remaining dough.

BAKE in preheated 375°F. oven for 10 to 12 minutes or until edges are golden brown. Let stand for 5 minutes; remove to wire racks to cool completely.

DECORATE cookies with frosting, remaining morsels, icing and assorted candies. Makes 10 large cookies.

Easy Butterscotch Chip Cookies

1 package (18½ ounces) chocolate cake mix
½ cup vegetable oil
2 eggs
1⅔ cups (11-ounce package) NESTLÉ® TOLL HOUSE®
    Butterscotch Morsels
½ cup chopped pecans (optional)

COMBINE chocolate cake mix, oil and eggs in large bowl. Stir in morsels and pecans, if desired. Drop by rounded tablespoon onto ungreased baking sheets.

BAKE in preheated 350°F. oven for 8 to 10 minutes or until centers are just set. Let stand for 2 minutes; remove to wire racks to cool completely. Makes about 3½ dozen cookies.

Double Chocolate Peanut Butter Thumbprint Cookies

1½ cups all-purpose flour

⅓ cup NESTLÉ® TOLL HOUSE® Baking Cocoa

1½ teaspoons baking powder

¼ teaspoon salt

2 cups (12-ounce package) NESTLÉ® TOLL HOUSE® Semi-Sweet Chocolate Morsels, *divided*

1 cup granulated sugar

About 1 cup chunky or creamy peanut butter (not all-natural), *divided*

⅓ cup butter or margarine, softened

1½ teaspoons vanilla extract

2 eggs

COMBINE flour, cocoa, baking powder and salt in small bowl. Melt 1 cup morsels in small, heavy-duty saucepan over lowest possible heat, stirring constantly until smooth.

BEAT granulated sugar, ⅓ cup peanut butter, butter and vanilla extract in large mixer bowl until creamy. Beat in melted chocolate. Add eggs, one at a time, beating well after each addition. Gradually beat in flour mixture. Stir in remaining morsels. Cover; chill just until firm.

SHAPE dough into 1½-inch balls. Place balls on ungreased baking sheets. Press ½-inch deep centers with thumb. Fill each center with about ½ teaspoon peanut butter.

BAKE in preheated 350°F. oven for 10 to 15 minutes or until sides are set but centers are still slightly soft. Let stand for 2 minutes; remove to wire racks to cool completely. Makes about 3½ dozen cookies.

Let the Kids In on the Fun!

Introducing kids to the delight of baking is not only a great indoor activity to keep them busy, but a way to teach skills they'll use throughout their lives. If you're looking for a fun, foolproof recipe for your first baking project, try Extra-Easy Cutout Cookies (see below).

Start by structuring the baking sessions so the children can do the "fun parts" without getting bored with the tedious tasks. For example, make doughs or frostings ahead so youngsters can jump right into cutting out cookies or frosting bars.

Tailor the children's involvement to suit their ages and interests. Young kids can roll dough into balls, push down on cookie cutters or sprinkle on simple toppings. Older children can assemble and mix batters or doughs, spread on frostings or position decorations. Preteens can do more involved tasks, such as sculpting dough, piping icing or preparing an entire recipe with minimal help.

To get started, involve your children by encouraging them to bake treats for special occasions. Allow them to choose what they'd like to make—for example, cutout snowmen or brownies. Then, choose recipes that are appropriate to their ability levels. Opt for simple recipes for preschoolers and save more elaborate ones for pre-teens.

Extra-Easy Cutout Cookies

The holidays wouldn't be the same without a batch of whimsically decorated cutout cookies. Short on time? No problem! Start with NESTLÉ® TOLL HOUSE® Refrigerated Chocolate Chip Cookie Dough and your favorite cookie cutters. These quick-fix cookies bake in just 6 to 9 minutes. To decorate the cooled cookies, use purchased or homemade vanilla frosting tinted with food coloring. For a thinner, glazelike topping, stir a small amount of light corn syrup into prepared frosting. Finish the cookies with your choice of candies or colored sugars.

Candy Shop Pizza

1 package (18 ounces) refrigerated NESTLÉ® TOLL HOUSE®
   Chocolate Chip Cookie Dough
1 cup (6 ounces) NESTLÉ® TOLL HOUSE® Semi-Sweet
   Chocolate Morsels
½ cup creamy or chunky peanut butter
1 cup coarsely chopped assorted candy bars

PRESS cookie dough evenly into bottom of greased 12-inch pizza
pan or 13 x 9-inch baking pan.

BAKE in preheated 350°F. oven for 14 to 18 minutes or until edge
is set and center is still slightly soft. Immediately sprinkle morsels
over hot crust; drop peanut butter by spoonfuls onto morsels. Let
stand for 5 minutes or until morsels become shiny and soft. Gently
spread chocolate and peanut butter evenly over cookie crust.

SPRINKLE candy in single layer over pizza. Cut into wedges; serve
warm or at room temperature. Makes 12 servings.

Heading for the Kitchen

Although your children may be anxious to begin baking, things will go more
smoothly if you take a few minutes to go over some basics. Make a game of
rolling up sleeves, tying back long hair, washing hands and putting on an apron.
Show your children how to use pot holders or hot pads for hot pans. Also, caution
them never to set hot pans and utensils directly on the counter, but to place them
on a hot pad or wire cooling rack instead. Finally, explain how to use scissors and
knives safely. Now you're ready to get on to the real fun—mixing up and baking
delicious cookies.

Spiderweb Munch

2 cups (12-ounce package) NESTLÉ® TOLL HOUSE®
  Semi-Sweet Chocolate Morsels
1 cup creamy peanut butter, *divided*
⅓ cup powdered sugar
3 cups toasted rice cereal

HEAT morsels and ¾ cup peanut butter in small, heavy-duty saucepan over low heat, stirring constantly until smooth; remove from heat. Add powdered sugar; stir vigorously until smooth.

PLACE cereal in large bowl. Add 1 cup melted chocolate mixture; stir until all cereal is coated. Place on ungreased baking sheet. Using small metal spatula, shape into 10-inch circle with slightly raised 1-inch-wide border. Pour remaining melted chocolate mixture in center of circle; spread to border.

For Spiderweb:
PLACE remaining peanut butter in heavy-duty plastic bag. Cut a small hole in corner of bag; squeeze to pipe peanut butter in concentric circles on top of chocolate. Using wooden pick or tip of sharp knife, pull tip through peanut butter from center to border. Chill for 30 minutes or until firm. Cut into wedges to serve. Makes 12 to 16 servings.

best of breads

savor the aroma of yeasty rolls, moist quick breads and scrumptious scones wafting from your very own oven. The following pages provide foolproof recipes for all of these and more. Wake up your family with hot-from-the-oven Pumpkin Swirl Breakfast Rolls. Looking for a bread to serve with soup? Bake a pan of Fiesta Corn Bread. Turn on the oven and pick one of the sweet or savory selections to serve with dinner tonight.

Pumpkin Cranberry Bread (see recipe, page 137)

Spiced Pumpkin Nut Bread

4 cups all-purpose flour
1 tablespoon pumpkin pie spice
2 teaspoons baking powder
1 teaspoon baking soda
¾ teaspoon salt
1¾ cup (15-ounce can) LIBBY'S® 100% Pure Pumpkin
2 cups packed brown sugar
1 cup apple juice
4 eggs
¼ cup vegetable oil
2 teaspoons vanilla extract
1 cup chopped nuts, *divided*

SIFT flour, pumpkin pie spice, baking powder, baking soda and salt into medium bowl. Combine pumpkin, brown sugar, apple juice, eggs, vegetable oil and vanilla extract in large bowl; stir well. Stir in flour mixture and ¾ cup nuts just until moistened. Spoon into two greased 9 x 5-inch loaf pans. Sprinkle remaining nuts over loaves.

BAKE in preheated 350°F. oven for 60 to 70 minutes or until wooden pick inserted in centers comes out clean. Cool in pans on wire rack for 10 minutes; remove to wire rack to cool completely. Makes 2 loaves.

Pumpkin Cranberry Bread

      3 cups all-purpose flour
      1 tablespoon plus 2 teaspoons pumpkin pie spice
      2 teaspoons baking soda
    1½ teaspoons salt
      3 cups granulated sugar
    1¾ cup (15-ounce can) LIBBY'S® 100% Pure Pumpkin
      4 eggs
      1 cup vegetable oil
    ½ cup orange juice or water
      1 cup sweetened dried, fresh or frozen cranberries

COMBINE flour, pumpkin pie spice, baking soda and salt in large bowl. Combine sugar, pumpkin, eggs, vegetable oil and orange juice in large mixer bowl; beat until just blended. Add pumpkin mixture to flour mixture; stir just until moistened. Fold in cranberries. Spoon batter into two greased 9 x 5-inch loaf pans.

BAKE in preheated 350°F. oven for 60 to 65 minutes or until wooden pick inserted in center comes out clean. Cool in pans on wire rack for 10 minutes; remove to wire racks to cool completely. Makes 2 loaves.

For Three 8 x 4-inch Loaf Pans:
PREPARE as directed. Bake for 55 to 60 minutes.

For Five or Six 5 x 3-Inch Mini Loaf Pans:
PREPARE as directed. Bake for 50 to 55 minutes.

Pictured on pages 134-135.

Pumpkin Swirl Breakfast Rolls

½ cup packed brown sugar

¾ teaspoon ground cinnamon

⅛ teaspoon ground cloves

⅓ cup butter or margarine

1 cup LIBBY'S® 100% Pure Pumpkin

¾ cup chopped walnuts or pecans

⅓ cup raisins

1 pound frozen bread dough, thawed

Glaze (recipe follows)

COMBINE brown sugar, cinnamon and cloves in medium bowl. Cut in butter with a pastry blender or 2 knives until crumbly. Stir in pumpkin, walnuts and raisins.

ROLL bread dough into 12 x 12-inch square;* spread with pumpkin mixture, leaving 1 inch border along 2 sides. Roll up dough, starting from side with 1-inch border; seal edges. Slice into 12 pieces; place cut sides up in greased 9-inch round or square baking pan. Let rise in warm place until double in size.

BAKE in preheated 375°F. oven for 20 to 25 minutes or until golden brown. Cool slightly on wire rack. Drizzle with Glaze. Serve warm. Makes 1 dozen rolls.

For Glaze:
COMBINE 1 cup sifted powdered sugar and 2 to 3 tablespoons water in small bowl until smooth.

*Note: For extra-large rolls, roll dough into 12 x 9-inch rectangle. Spread with pumpkin mixture, leaving 1-inch border along 9-inch sides. Roll up dough, starting from 9-inch side; seal edges. Slice into 6 pieces; place cut sides up in greased 9-inch baking pan. Let rise and bake as above. Makes ½ dozen rolls.

Pumpkin Nut Mini Loaves

3¼ cups all-purpose flour

¾ cup quick or old-fashioned oats

2 teaspoons baking soda

1½ teaspoons pumpkin pie spice

½ teaspoon baking powder

½ teaspoon salt

1¾ cup (15-ounce can) LIBBY'S® 100% Pure Pumpkin

1½ cups granulated sugar

1½ cups packed brown sugar

3 eggs

½ cup water

½ cup vegetable oil

½ cup NESTLÉ® CARNATION® Evaporated Milk

1 cup chopped walnuts

COMBINE flour, oats, baking soda, pumpkin pie spice, baking powder and salt in large bowl. Beat pumpkin, granulated sugar, brown sugar, eggs, water, vegetable oil and evaporated milk in large mixer bowl on medium speed until combined. Gradually beat flour mixture into pumpkin mixture on low speed; stir in walnuts. Spread into 6 greased 5 x 3-inch mini loaf pans.*

BAKE in preheated 350°F. oven for 40 to 45 minutes or until wooden pick inserted in centers comes out clean. Cool in pans on wire racks for 10 minutes. Remove to racks to cool completely. Makes 6 loaves.

*NOTE: To make regular-size loaves, prepared recipe and spread batter into 2 greased 9 x 5-inch loaf pans. Bake in preheated 350°F. oven for 65 to 70 minutes or until wooden pick inserted in centers comes out clean. Cool as above. Makes 2 loaves.

Pumpkin Honey Wheat Bread

2¼ cups all-purpose flour
¾ cup wheat germ
2½ teaspoons baking powder
1½ teaspoons ground cinnamon
1 teaspoon salt
½ teaspoon baking soda
1¼ cups LIBBY'S® 100% Pure Pumpkin
¾ cup honey
2 eggs
¼ cup vegetable oil
¼ cup milk
¼ cup pine nuts or sunflower seeds

COMBINE flour, wheat germ, baking powder, cinnamon, salt and baking soda in large bowl. Combine pumpkin, honey, eggs, vegetable oil and milk in medium bowl; add to flour mixture. Stir just until blended.

SPREAD batter into greased 9 x 5-inch loaf pan. Sprinkle with pine nuts; gently pat into batter. Bake in preheated 350°F. oven for 55 to 60 minutes or until wooden pick inserted in center comes out clean. Cool in pan on wire rack for 10 minutes; remove to wire rack to cool completely. Makes 1 loaf.

Quick Bread Savvy

With today's busy schedules, a quick bread is a smart choice whenever you want the fresh-from-the-oven goodness of homemade bread. With these helpful hints, you can enjoy scrumptious loaves and coffeecakes that look and taste as if they were made by an expert.

Start by measuring the ingredients accurately. Successful quick breads depend on the right amounts of ingredients. Too much or too little flour, liquid or leavening may cause trouble.

When you add the liquid ingredients to the dry ones, don't mix the batter too much. Stir only until the dry ingredients are just moistened with some tiny lumps. If you overmix, the bread may be tough and have tunnels.

Once the batter is in the pan, put it in the oven right away. Batters with baking powder and/or baking soda should be baked immediately or the leavening power will be lost.

Check the bread 10 to 15 minutes before the end of the baking. If the bread seems to be browning too quickly, cover it lightly with foil. A crack down the center of a loaf is typical and shows that the batter has risen properly.

To test if a quick bread is done, insert a wooden pick near the center of the bread. If the pick comes out clean, the bread is done. If not, bake it a few minutes more and test again.

Cool a quick bread in the pan on a wire rack about 10 minutes. Then, remove it from the pan and continue cooling it on the rack. The rack allows air to circulate under the bread so it won't become soggy.

While a coffeecake is best served warm, a quick bread loaf improves with standing. If you let it stand overnight, the flavors will have a chance to mellow, and the bread won't crumble when you slice it. After baking, let the loaf cool completely on a wire rack. Wrap it tightly in foil and store it overnight at room temperature. For longer storage, keep it in the refrigerator for up to a week. You can freeze a quick bread for up to 3 months. Place the completely cooled loaf in a freezer container or bag. Before serving, thaw the wrapped loaf overnight in the refrigerator.

Pumpkin Banana Nut Bread

4 cups all-purpose flour
4 teaspoons baking powder
4 teaspoons ground cinnamon
2 teaspoons ground ginger
2 teaspoons baking soda
½ teaspoon salt
1 can (15 ounces) LIBBY'S® 100% Pure Pumpkin
4 eggs
1 cup granulated sugar
1 cup packed brown sugar
1 cup (about 2 medium) mashed very ripe bananas
¾ cup vegetable oil
1 cup chopped walnuts

COMBINE flour, baking powder, cinnamon, ginger, baking soda and salt in medium bowl. Combine pumpkin, eggs, granulated sugar, brown sugar, bananas and vegetable oil in large mixer bowl; beat until smooth. Gradually beat in flour mixture; stir in nuts.

SPOON into two greased and floured 9 x 5-inch loaf pans. Bake in preheated 350° F. oven for 55 to 60 minutes or until wooden pick inserted in centers comes out clean. Cool in pans on wire rack for 10 minutes. Remove to wire racks to cool completely. Makes 2 loaves.

Iced Nut and Pumpkin Loaf

1¾ cups all-purpose flour
½ cup pecans, finely chopped or ground
2¼ teaspoons pumpkin pie spice
1 teaspoon baking soda
½ teaspoon salt
1 cup (2 sticks) butter or margarine, softened
¾ cup granulated sugar
½ cup packed brown sugar
3 eggs
1 cup LIBBY'S® 100% Pure Pumpkin
Icing (recipe follows)

COMBINE flour, pecans, pumpkin pie spice, baking soda and salt in medium bowl. Beat butter, granulated sugar and brown sugar in large mixer bowl until creamy. Beat in eggs until light and fluffy. Gradually beat in pumpkin and flour mixture.

POUR into greased and floured 9 x 5-inch loaf pan. Bake in preheated 325°F. oven for 1 hour and 15 minutes or until wooden pick inserted in center comes out clean. Cool in pan on wire rack for 10 minutes; remove to wire rack to cool completely.

SPREAD Icing over top of loaf, allowing some to drizzle down sides.* Makes 1 loaf.

For Icing:
COMBINE 1¼ cups sifted powdered sugar and 3 to 4 teaspoons water in small bowl.

*Note: To make design, place 2 tablespoons Icing in small, heavy-duty plastic bag. Tint with 1 drop maple flavoring or vanilla extract; knead until blended. Cut a small hole in corner of bag; squeeze to drizzle over loaf in crisscross design.

Pumpkin Marmalade Bread

2¼ cups all-purpose flour
¾ cup packed brown sugar
¾ cup granulated sugar
4½ teaspoons pumpkin pie spice
2¼ teaspoons baking powder
¾ teaspoon ground cinnamon
¼ teaspoon salt
1¼ cups LIBBY'S® 100% Pure Pumpkin
4 eggs
½ cup (1 stick) butter or margarine, melted
⅓ cup orange marmalade
3 tablespoons orange liqueur or orange juice
Marmalade Glaze (recipe follows)

COMBINE flour, brown sugar, granulated sugar, pumpkin pie spice, baking powder, cinnamon and salt in medium bowl. Beat pumpkin, eggs, butter, marmalade and liqueur in a large mixer bowl until blended. Gradually beat in flour mixture.

SPREAD batter into greased 9 x 5-inch loaf pan. Bake in preheated 350°F. oven for 65 to 70 minutes or until wooden pick inserted in center comes out clean. Cool in pan on wire rack for 10 minutes; remove to wire rack to cool completely. Spread with Marmalade Glaze. Makes 1 loaf.

For Marmalade Glaze:
MIX 2 tablespoons orange marmalade and 1 tablespoon orange liqueur or orange juice in small bowl.

Old-Fashioned Nut Loaf

  2 cups all-purpose flour
  2 teaspoons baking powder
  2 teaspoons pumpkin pie spice
  1 teaspoon salt
  ½ teaspoon baking soda
1½ cups LIBBY'S® 100% Pure Pumpkin
  ½ cup granulated sugar
  ½ cup packed brown sugar
  ½ cup NESTLÉ® CARNATION® Evaporated Fat Free Milk
  1 egg
  1 egg white
  1 tablespoon vegetable oil
  ¼ cup chopped nuts

COMBINE flour, baking powder, pumpkin pie spice, salt and baking soda in medium bowl. Combine pumpkin, granulated sugar, brown sugar, evaporated fat free milk, egg, egg white and vegetable oil in large bowl. Stir in flour mixture until just moistened. Spread batter into greased 9 x 5-inch loaf pan. Sprinkle batter with nuts.

BAKE in preheated 350°F. oven for 60 to 65 minutes or until wooden pick inserted in center comes out clean. Cool in pan on wire rack for 10 minutes. Remove to wire rack to cool completely. Makes 1 loaf.

Pumpkin Apple Gingerbread

3½ cups all-purpose flour

1 tablespoon baking powder

2½ teaspoons ground ginger

½ teaspoon baking soda

½ teaspoon salt

½ teaspoon pumpkin pie spice

1 cup (2 sticks) butter or margarine, softened

1 cup granulated sugar

½ cup packed brown sugar

4 eggs

1¾ cup (15-ounce can) LIBBY'S® 100% Pure Pumpkin

1 large baking apple (such as Granny Smith), peeled, cored and shredded (about 1 cup)

½ cup molasses

Sifted powdered sugar

Hard Sauce (recipe follows)

COMBINE flour, baking powder, ginger, baking soda, salt and pumpkin pie spice in medium bowl.

BEAT butter, granulated sugar and brown sugar in large mixer bowl until light and fluffy. Add eggs, two at a time, beating well after each addition. Beat in pumpkin, apple and molasses. Gradually beat in flour mixture.

SPOON batter into well-greased and floured 12-cup fluted tube pan.* Bake in preheated 350°F. oven for 1 hour or until wooden pick inserted in center comes out clean. Cool in pan on wire rack for 15 minutes; remove from pan. Dust with powdered sugar. Serve warm with Hard Sauce. Makes 12 servings.

For Hard Sauce:
BEAT 1 cup (2 sticks) softened butter and 2 teaspoons vanilla extract in small mixer bowl until smooth. Gradually beat in 4 cups sifted powdered sugar until fluffy.

*Note: Recipe also may be made in two greased and floured 8- or 9-inch round cake pans or one 13 x 9-inch baking pan. Bake in preheated 350°F. oven for 40 to 45 minutes or until wooden pick inserted in center comes out clean.

Pumpkin Scones

2½ cups all-purpose flour
¼ cup packed brown sugar
1 tablespoon baking powder
1 teaspoon ground cinnamon
½ teaspoon salt
¼ teaspoon ground cloves
½ cup shortening
¾ cup LIBBY'S® 100% Pure Pumpkin
½ cup milk

COMBINE flour, brown sugar, baking powder, cinnamon, salt and cloves in large bowl. Cut in shortening with pastry blender or 2 knives until mixture resembles coarse crumbs. Combine pumpkin and milk in small bowl. Add to flour mixture; mix just until dough forms.

KNEAD dough gently on floured surface 10 to 12 times. Pat half of dough into a 7-inch circle; cut into 6 to 8 wedges. Repeat with remaining dough. Place wedges 2 inches apart on ungreased baking sheet.

BAKE in preheated 450°F. oven for 12 to 14 minutes or until light golden color. Remove scones to wire rack; cool slightly. Serve warm. Makes 12 to 16 scones.

Southwestern Biscuits

2¼ cups all-purpose flour
2 tablespoons granulated sugar
1 tablespoon baking powder
3 tablespoons butter or margarine, softened
1 egg
1 cup (8-ounce can) cream-style corn
½ cup (4-ounce can) ORTEGA® Diced Green Chiles
1 tablespoon chopped fresh cilantro (optional)

COMBINE flour, sugar and baking powder in large bowl. Add butter; cut in with pastry blender or 2 knives until mixture resembles coarse crumbs.

STIR IN egg, corn, chiles and, if desired, cilantro; combine just until mixture holds together. Knead dough 10 times on well-floured surface. Pat dough to ¾-inch thickness. Cut into 3-inch biscuits. Place on greased baking sheet.

BAKE in preheated 400°F. oven for 20 to 25 minutes or until wooden pick inserted in center comes out clean. Cool on baking sheet for 5 minutes; remove to wire racks to cool completely. Makes about 8 biscuits.

Bake a Better Biscuit

Making light, tender and flaky biscuits is easy if you remember these basics:

Cut in the butter or margarine just until the flour mixture resembles coarse crumbs. Then, stir in the liquid only until the ingredients are just moistened.

Knead the dough lightly by folding and pressing only enough to distribute the liquid; 10 strokes is plenty.

Cut out as many biscuits as possible from the first rolling of dough. Additional rolling and extra flour will make the biscuits tough and dry.

Place biscuits close together on the baking sheet for a soft crust; for a firmer crust, place them about 1 inch apart.

Fiesta Corn Bread

2¼ cups all-purpose flour

1¼ cups ALBERS® Corn Meal

1½ cups (6 ounces) shredded cheddar cheese

1 cup (7 ounce can) ORTEGA® Diced Green Chiles

½ cup granulated sugar

2 tablespoons baking powder

1½ teaspoons salt

2 cups milk

⅔ cup vegetable oil

2 eggs, lightly beaten

COMBINE flour, corn meal, cheese, chiles, sugar, baking powder and salt in large bowl. Add milk, oil and eggs; stir just until moistened. Spread into greased 13 x 9-inch baking pan.

BAKE in preheated 375°F. oven for 30 to 35 minutes or until wooden pick inserted in center comes out clean. Cool in pan for 10 minutes; cut into 12 squares. Cut squares diagonally in half. Makes 24 servings.

Golden Herb Rolls

⅔ cup milk

½ cup (1 stick) butter or margarine

¼ cup water

4 cups all-purpose flour, *divided*

⅓ cup granulated sugar

1 package quick-rising yeast

2 teaspoons dried savory leaves, crushed

1 teaspoon salt

¾ teaspoon dried thyme leaves, crushed

½ teaspoon dried dill, crushed

1 cup LIBBY'S® 100% Pure Pumpkin

4 eggs, *divided*

2 tablespoons sesame seeds

COMBINE milk, butter and water in small saucepan; heat until butter is melted. If necessary, cool to 120°F. to 130°F. Combine 3 cups flour, sugar, yeast, savory, salt, thyme and dill in large mixer bowl. Add milk mixture and pumpkin; beat for 2 minutes. Stir in 3 eggs and remaining flour.

COVER; let rise in warm, draft-free place for 10 minutes or until doubled. Spoon into 20 to 24 well-greased muffin cups, filling ½ to ¾ full. Cover; let rise in warm, draft-free place for 30 to 40 minutes or until doubled. Beat remaining egg and brush on top of rolls; sprinkle with sesame seeds.

BAKE in preheated 350°F. oven for 30 to 40 minutes or until golden and rolls sound hollow when tapped. Remove from pans; serve warm, or cool on wire rack. Makes 20 to 24 rolls.

cakes

luscious layer cakes, cute-as-a-button cupcakes and buttery tube cakes mark birthdays, anniversaries and many other celebrations. In this chapter, you'll find cakes for all occasions, from towering Vermont Spice Cake to personal-sized Glazed Chocolate Sweet Cakes. Pumpkin Pecan Rum Cake completes a holiday meal with festive and traditional flavors. And for everyday desserts, bake our extra-easy Pumpkin Crunch Cake.

Cinnamon Chocolate Cake (*see recipe, page 158*)

Cinnamon Chocolate Cake

CHOCOLATE CAKE:
- 1 cup (6 ounces) NESTLÉ® TOLL HOUSE® Semi-Sweet Chocolate Morsels
- 1¼ cups granulated sugar
- ¾ cup (1½ sticks) butter or margarine, softened
- 1 teaspoon vanilla extract
- 3 eggs
- 2 cups all-purpose flour
- 1 tablespoon ground cinnamon
- 1 teaspoon baking soda
- ½ teaspoon salt
- 1 cup milk
- 1 to 2 tablespoons ORTEGA® Diced Jalapeños (optional)

CHOCOLATE FROSTING:
- 3 to 3¼ cups sifted powdered sugar
- ½ cup milk
- ¼ cup (½ stick) butter or margarine, softened
- 2 packets (1 ounce each) NESTLÉ® TOLL HOUSE® CHOCO BAKE® Unsweetened Chocolate Flavor
- 2 teaspoons vanilla extract
- ¼ teaspoon salt
- 1¼ cups sliced almonds, toasted

For Chocolate Cake:
MICROWAVE morsels in medium, microwave-safe bowl on HIGH (100%) power for 1 minute; stir. Microwave at additional 10- to 20- second intervals, stirring until smooth. Beat sugar, butter and vanilla extract in large mixer bowl. Add eggs; beat for 1 minute. Beat in melted chocolate. Combine flour, cinnamon, baking soda and salt in medium bowl; beat into chocolate mixture alternately with milk. Stir in jalapeños, if desired. Pour into 2 well greased 9-inch round cake pans.

BAKE in preheated 350°F. oven for 30 to 35 minutes or until wooden pick inserted in center comes out clean. Cool in pans on wire racks for 20 minutes. Invert onto wire racks to cool completely.

For Chocolate Frosting:
BEAT powdered sugar, milk, butter, Choco Bake, vanilla extract and salt in small mixer bowl until mixture is smooth and creamy. Frost cake. Decorate sides with nuts. Makes 12 servings.
Pictured on pages 156-157.

Pumpkin Pecan Rum Cake

¾ cup chopped pecans
3 cups all-purpose flour
2 tablespoons pumpkin pie spice
2 teaspoons baking soda
1 teaspoon salt
1¼ cups (2½ sticks) butter or margarine, softened, *divided*
1½ cups granulated sugar, *divided*
1 cup packed brown sugar
4 eggs
1¾ cups (15-ounce can) LIBBY'S® 100% Pure Pumpkin
1 teaspoon vanilla extract
2 tablespoons water
2 to 3 tablespoons dark rum or 1 teaspoon rum extract

GREASE 12-cup tube pan. Sprinkle pecans over bottom.

COMBINE flour, pumpkin pie spice, baking soda and salt in medium bowl. Beat 1 cup butter, 1 cup granulated sugar and brown sugar in large mixer bowl until light and fluffy. Add eggs; beat well. Add pumpkin and vanilla extract; beat well. Add flour mixture to pumpkin mixture, one-third at a time, mixing well after each addition. Spoon batter into prepared pan.

BAKE in preheated 325°F. oven for 60 to 70 minutes or until wooden pick inserted in center comes out clean. Cool 10 minutes.

MELT remaining butter in small saucepan; stir in remaining granulated sugar and water. Bring to a boil. Remove from heat; stir in rum or rum extract. Make holes in cake with long pick; pour half of rum mixture over cake. Let stand 5 minutes and invert onto plate. Make holes in top of cake; pour remaining rum mixture over cake. Cool. Garnish as desired. Makes 24 servings.

Pumpkin White Chunk Cake

- 3 cups buttermilk baking mix
- 1½ cups granulated sugar
- 2½ teaspoons ground cinnamon
- 1 cup LIBBY'S® 100% Pure Pumpkin
- 2 eggs, lightly beaten
- ½ cup water

- 2 teaspoons vanilla extract
- 3 bars (one 6-ounce box) NESTLÉ® TOLL HOUSE® Premier White Baking Bars, coarsely chopped, *divided*
- ⅔ cup chopped pecans, *divided*

STIR together baking mix, sugar and cinnamon in large bowl. Stir in pumpkin, eggs, water and vanilla extract just until moistened. Stir in half of baking bars and half of pecans. Spread into greased 13 x 9-inch baking pan.

BAKE in preheated 350°F. oven for 20 minutes. Sprinkle with remaining baking bars and remaining pecans. Bake for 10 to 15 minutes or until wooden pick inserted in center comes out clean. Cool completely in pan on wire rack. Makes 16 servings.

Quick Pumpkin Cupcakes

1 package (16 ounces) pound cake mix
1 cup LIBBY'S® 100% Pure Pumpkin
2 eggs
⅓ cup water
2 teaspoons pumpkin pie spice
1 teaspoon baking soda
1 container (16 ounces) prepared vanilla frosting
12 to 14 whole walnut halves

BEAT cake mix, pumpkin, eggs, water, pumpkin pie spice and baking soda in large mixer bowl on medium speed for 3 minutes. Pour batter into 12 to 14 paper-lined muffin cups.

BAKE in preheated 325°F. oven for 25 to 30 minutes or until golden brown. Cool in pan on wire rack for 10 minutes. Remove to wire rack to cool completely. Spread cupcakes with frosting. Top with walnut halves. Makes 12 to 14 cupcakes.

Grease It Right

To grease cake pans just enough, but not too much, spread on the shortening with a paper towel and use about 1 teaspoon for an 8- or 9-inch round cake pan and 1½ to 2 teaspoons for 13 x 9-inch baking pan or a 15 x 10-inch jelly-roll pan. If you want to leave the cake in the pan for serving, grease only the bottom. If you plan to remove the cake from the pan, grease and flour both the bottom and sides of the pan. To flour a pan, sprinkle a little flour into the pan once you've greased it. Then, tilt and tap the pan so the flour covers all the greased surfaces. Tap out any excess flour.

Vermont Spice Cake

CAKE:

- 1½ cups granulated sugar
- ¾ cup (1½ sticks) butter, softened
- 3 eggs
- 1½ cups LIBBY'S® 100% Pure Pumpkin
- 1½ teaspoons vanilla extract
- ½ cup NESTLÉ® CARNATION® Evaporated Milk
- ¼ cup water
- 3 cups all-purpose flour
- 3½ teaspoons baking powder
- 1½ teaspoons ground cinnamon
- 1 teaspoon baking soda
- ¾ teaspoon ground nutmeg
- ½ teaspoon salt
- ¼ teaspoon ground cloves
- ¼ teaspoon ground ginger
  Chopped nuts and/or nut halves (optional)

MAPLE FROSTING:

- 1 package (8 ounces) and 1 package (3 ounces) cream cheese, softened
- ⅓ cup butter, softened
- 3½ cups sifted powdered sugar
- 2 to 3 teaspoons maple flavoring

For Cake:

BEAT sugar and butter in large mixer bowl until creamy. Add eggs; beat for 2 minutes. Add pumpkin and vanilla extract; mix well. Beat in evaporated milk and water.

COMBINE flour, baking powder, cinnamon, baking soda, nutmeg, salt, cloves and ginger in a large bowl. Beat into pumpkin mixture.

SPREAD pumpkin mixture evenly into 2 greased and floured 9-inch round cake pans. Bake in preheated 325°F. oven for 35 to 40 minutes or until wooden pick inserted in center comes out clean. Cool in pans on wire racks for 15 minutes. Invert onto wire racks to cool completely.

For Maple Frosting:

BEAT cream cheese and butter in large mixer bowl; gradually beat in powdered sugar. Beat in maple flavoring until fluffy.

To Assemble:

CUT cakes in half horizontally with long serrated knife. Frost between layers and on top of cake, leaving sides unfrosted. Top with nuts, if desired. Store in refrigerator. Makes 12 servings.

Glazed Chocolate Sweet Cakes

CAKES:
- 2 cups (12-ounce package) NESTLÉ® TOLL HOUSE® Semi-Sweet Chocolate Morsels, *divided*
- 1½ cups all-purpose flour
- 1 teaspoon baking soda
- 1 teaspoon salt
- ½ cup granulated sugar
- ⅓ cup vegetable oil
- 1 egg
- 1 teaspoon vanilla extract
- 1 cup water

GLAZE:
- ⅔ cup heavy whipping cream
- 2 tablespoons butter or margarine
- 2 tablespoons light corn syrup
- Sweetened whipped cream (optional)
- Orange peel curls (optional)

For Cakes:

MICROWAVE 1 cup morsels in small, microwave-safe bowl on HIGH (100%) power for 1 minute; stir. Microwave at additional 10- to 20- second intervals, stirring until smooth. Cool to room temperature. Combine flour, baking soda and salt in small bowl.

BEAT sugar, oil, egg and vanilla extract in large mixer bowl until blended. Beat in melted chocolate. Gradually beat in flour mixture alternately with water. Spoon into 12 greased muffin cups.

BAKE in preheated 350°F. oven for 18 to 22 minutes or until wooden pick inserted in center comes out clean. Let stand for 20 minutes. Remove from pan; turn upside down on wire rack to cool completely. Trim edges with scissors, if necessary.

For Glaze:

HEAT remaining morsels, cream, butter and corn syrup in medium, heavy-duty saucepan over medium heat until mixture comes to a boil, stirring constantly. Remove from heat; stir until smooth. Cool to room temperature. Spread over sides and flat tops of cakes or dip cakes into glaze. Garnish with whipped cream and orange peel curls just before serving, if desired. Makes 12 mini cakes.

Marbled Chocolate
Sour Cream Cake

1 cup (6 ounces) NESTLÉ® TOLL HOUSE® Semi-Sweet
   Chocolate Morsels
1 package (18½ ounces) yellow cake mix
4 eggs
¾ cup sour cream
½ cup vegetable oil
¼ cup water
¼ cup granulated sugar
   Powdered sugar

MICROWAVE morsels in medium, microwave-safe bowl on HIGH
(100%) power for 1 minute; stir. Microwave at additional 10- to
20-second intervals, stirring until smooth.

COMBINE cake mix, eggs, sour cream, oil, water and granulated
sugar in large mixer bowl. Beat on low speed until moistened. Beat
on high speed for 2 minutes.

STIR 2 cups batter into melted chocolate. Alternately spoon
batters into greased 10-cup fluted or or round tube pan.

BAKE in preheated 375°F. oven for 35 to 45 minutes or until
wooden pick inserted in center comes out clean. Cool in pan on
wire rack for 20 minutes. Invert onto wire rack to cool completely.
Sprinkle with powdered sugar before serving. Makes 24 servings.

Pumpkin Orange Cake Roll

CAKE ROLL:
1   package (16 ounces) angel food cake mix
2½ teaspoons grated orange peel, *divided*
½   cup powdered sugar

FILLING:
1½ cups LIBBY'S® 100% Pure Pumpkin
½   cup granulated sugar
1   teaspoon ground cinnamon
1   teaspoon vanilla extract
    Sifted powdered sugar
2   tablespoons currant or grape jelly

For Cake Roll:
PREPARE cake mix according to package directions, adding 1½ teaspoons orange peel at end of mixing time. Spread batter evenly into foil-lined 15 x 10-inch jelly-roll pan. (Foil should extend 1 inch above edge of pan.)

BAKE at oven temperature specified in package directions for 30 minutes or until top of cake springs back when touched. While cake is baking, sprinkle a kitchen towel with powdered sugar. Immediately turn cake out onto towel. Carefully peel off foil. Roll up cake and towel together, starting with a narrow end. Cool on wire rack.

For Filling:
COMBINE pumpkin, granulated sugar, cinnamon, vanilla extract and remaining orange peel in medium bowl.

To Assemble:
CAREFULLY unroll cake and spread with Filling. Reroll cake. Sprinkle with powdered sugar. Stir jelly well; spoon into small, heavy-duty plastic bag. Cut a small hole in corner of bag; squeeze to drizzle jelly over cake roll. Makes 10 servings.

Pumpkin Orange Poppy Seed Cake

1 package (18¼ ounces) yellow cake mix
1¼ cups LIBBY'S® 100% Pure Pumpkin
⅔ cup orange juice
3 eggs
¼ cup poppy seeds
Orange Glaze (recipe follows)
Low-fat frozen yogurt (optional)

COMBINE cake mix, pumpkin, orange juice and eggs in large mixer bowl; beat on low speed for 30 seconds. Beat on medium speed for 2 minutes. Add poppy seeds; mix until blended. Spread batter into greased and floured 12-cup fluted tube pan.

BAKE in preheated 350°F. oven for 35 to 40 minutes or until wooden pick inserted in cake comes out clean. Cool in pan on wire rack for 10 minutes. Invert onto wire rack to cool completely. Frost top of cake with Orange Glaze. If desired, serve with frozen yogurt. Makes 24 servings.

For Orange Glaze:
COMBINE 1½ cups sifted powdered sugar and 2 to 3 tablespoons orange juice in small bowl until smooth.

Add Pumpkin, Cut the Fat

Add flavor and minimize the fat in packaged muffin and cake mixes! Simply replace the oil called for in the package directions with an equal amount of pumpkin. The result is a moist and delicious cake or muffin with less fat. Adding pumpkin to mixes in place of the fat also results in a wonderful moist texture. To taste for yourself, try the Pumpkin Orange Poppy Seed Cake. Because the pumpkin keeps it moist, this cake tastes every bit as good the second day!

Pumpkin Crunch Cake

  1 package (18¼ ounces) yellow cake mix, *divided*
1⅔ cups LIBBY'S® Easy Pumpkin Pie Mix
  2 eggs
  2 teaspoons pumpkin pie spice
 ⅓ cup flaked coconut
 ¼ cup chopped nuts
  3 tablespoons butter or margarine, softened

COMBINE 3 cups dry cake mix, pumpkin pie mix, eggs and pumpkin pie spice in large mixer bowl until moistened. Beat on medium speed for 2 minutes. Spread batter into greased 13 x 9-inch baking pan.

COMBINE remaining dry cake mix, coconut and nuts in small bowl; cut in butter with pastry blender or 2 knives until crumbly. Sprinkle mixture over batter.

BAKE in preheated 350°F. oven for 30 to 35 minutes or until wooden pick inserted in center comes out clean. Cool in pan on wire rack. Makes 20 servings.

Special Finishing Touches

A dusting of powdered sugar or a sprinkling of nuts can turn the most basic dessert into a showpiece. Count on these simple garnishing ideas to dress up your pies, cakes and other baked goods.

Edible flowers, including nasturtiums, pansies and violets, offer simple elegance on desserts or on dessert plates. Look for edible flowers in supermarkets or local gardens. Make sure they are chemical-free.

Turn to the fruit bowl for fresh and simple garnishes. Strawberry fans, thinly sliced citrus, assorted berries and kiwi fruit wedges add bursts of color and flavor, too.

For easy drizzling with no mess, create a makeshift pastry bag from a heavy-duty self sealing plastic bag. To drizzle chocolate, snip a small hole in a corner of a bag filled with melted NESTLÉ® TOLL HOUSE® Morsels (see Masterful Melting, page 234). Use to write, design or draw, decorating desserts or plates in your own creative way. This makeshift pastry bag works well for icing and jelly designs, too.

Press handfuls of chopped nuts along the sides of a frosted cake or sprinkle them on top. Whole nuts, caramelized nuts and chocolate-dipped nuts also jazz up desserts.

Add the look of lace or a stenciled design on cakes with doilies or stencils. Lay the doily or stencil on top of the cake and gently sift powdered sugar or unsweetened cocoa over the top. Carefully remove the doily or stencil to see your work of art. For a striped or checkerboard design, position strips of waxed paper on the cake and repeat as above.

Pumpkin Carrot Cake

2 cups all-purpose flour
2 teaspoons baking soda
2 teaspoons ground cinnamon
½ teaspoon salt
¾ cup milk
1½ teaspoons lemon juice
1½ cups granulated sugar
1¼ cups LIBBY'S® 100% Pure Pumpkin
3 eggs

½ cup packed brown sugar
½ cup vegetable oil
1 cup (8-ounce can) crushed pineapple, drained
1 cup grated carrots (about 3 medium)
1 cup flaked coconut
1¼ cups chopped walnuts, *divided*
Cream Cheese Frosting (recipe follows)

COMBINE flour, baking soda, cinnamon and salt in small bowl. Combine milk and lemon juice in liquid measuring cup (mixture will appear curdled).

BEAT granulated sugar, pumpkin, eggs, brown sugar and vegetable oil in large mixer bowl until combined. Beat in pineapple, carrots and milk mixture until combined. Gradually beat in flour mixture. Stir in coconut and 1 cup walnuts. Pour into 2 greased 9-inch round cake pans.

BAKE in preheated 350°F. oven for 30 to 35 minutes or until wooden pick inserted in center comes out clean. Cool in pans on wire racks for 15 minutes. Remove to racks to cool completely.

To Assemble:
To Assemble: Frost between layers, top and sides with Cream Cheese Frosting. Garnish side of cake with remaining walnuts. Store in refrigerator. Makes 12 servings.

For Cream Cheese Frosting:
BEAT 1 package (8 ounces) and 1 package (3 ounces) softened cream cheese and ⅓ cup softened butter in large mixer bowl; gradually beat in 3½ cups sifted powdered sugar. Beat in 2 teaspoons orange juice, 1 teaspoon vanilla extract and 1 teaspoon grated orange peel until fluffy.

pies and tarts

show off your baking talents with one of these elegant tarts or old-fashioned pies. Even if you're a newcomer to baking, you can turn out perfect pies with these easy recipes. Vary the pumpkin pie theme by serving Sour Cream Orange Pumpkin Pie or Walnut Crunch Pumpkin Pie. Chocolate lovers can indulge in wedges of ultra-rich Chocolate Truffle Tart. Choose a recipe, roll up your sleeves and roll out the dough. It's that easy!

Pumpkin Pecan Pie (see recipe, page 180)

Pumpkin Pecan Pie

1 unbaked 9-inch (4-cup volume) deep-dish pie shell (see recipe, *page 194*)
3 eggs, *divided*
1 cup LIBBY'S® 100% Pure Pumpkin
⅓ cup plus ½ cup granulated sugar, *divided*
1 teaspoon pumpkin pie spice
⅔ cup light corn syrup
3 tablespoons butter or margarine, melted
½ teaspoon vanilla extract
1 cup pecan halves
   Vanilla ice cream (optional)

COMBINE 1 egg, pumpkin, ⅓ cup sugar, and pumpkin pie spice in medium bowl. Spread over bottom of pie shell.

COMBINE corn syrup, remaining eggs, ½ cup sugar, butter and vanilla extract in medium bowl; stir in pecans. Spoon over pumpkin layer.

*BAKE in preheated 350°F. oven for 50 minutes or until filling is set. Cook on wire rack. If desired, serve with ice cream. Makes 8 servings.

*Note: If using a metal or foil pan, bake on preheated, heavy-duty baking sheet.

Pictured on pages 178 and 179.

Libby's® Pumpkin Brings Pure Pleasure

Since 1929, people who love to bake have enjoyed the convenience, rich flavor and perfect texture of Libby's® 100% Pure Pumpkin. Year after year, they've relied on this all-natural product to bring out the best in their favorite recipes.

At Libby's, not just any pumpkin will do. After years of research, Libby's developed its own superior breed of the Dickinson pumpkin. Called the Libby's Select, this sweet and meaty pumpkin boasts plenty of flavor, less water and a rich, golden color. This product ensures moist, sweet and fresh-tasting results time after time.

Walnut Crunch Pumpkin Pie

1	unbaked 9-inch (4-cup volume) deep-dish pie shell (see recipe, *page 194*)
1¼	cups coarsely chopped walnuts
¾	cup packed brown sugar
1¾	cups (15-ounce can) LIBBY'S® 100% Pure Pumpkin
1	can (12 fluid ounces) NESTLÉ® CARNATION® Evaporated Milk
¾	cup granulated sugar
2	eggs, lightly beaten
1	teaspoon ground cinnamon
½	teaspoon ground ginger
¼	teaspoon salt
¼	teaspoon ground cloves
3	tablespoons butter, melted

COMBINE walnuts and brown sugar in small bowl; place ¾ cup walnut mixture in bottom of pie shell. Reserve remaining walnut mixture. Combine pumpkin, evaporated milk, granulated sugar, eggs, cinnamon, ginger, salt and cloves in large bowl; mix well. Pour into pie shell.

BAKE in preheated 425°F. oven for 15 minutes. Reduce temperature to 350°F.; bake for 40 to 50 minutes or until knife inserted near center comes out clean. Cool on wire rack.

COMBINE butter with remaining walnut mixture; stir until moistened. Sprinkle over cooled pie. Broil at least 5 inches from the heat for 2 to 3 minutes or until bubbly. Cool on wire rack before serving. Makes 8 servings.

Carnation® Key Lime Pie

1 prepared 9-inch (9 ounces) graham cracker crust

1 can (14 ounces) NESTLÉ® CARNATION® Sweetened Condensed Milk

½ cup (about 3 medium limes) fresh lime juice

1 teaspoon grated lime peel

2 cups frozen whipped topping, thawed

BEAT sweetened condensed milk and lime juice in small mixer bowl until combined; stir in lime peel. Pour into crust; spread with whipped topping. Refrigerate for 2 hours or until set. Makes 8 servings.

Nestlé® Toll House® Chocolate Chip Pie

1 unbaked 9-inch (4-cup volume) deep-dish pie shell* (see
   recipe, *page 194*)
2 eggs
½ cup all-purpose flour
½ cup granulated sugar
½ cup packed brown sugar
¾ cup (1½ sticks) butter, softened
1 cup (6 ounces) NESTLÉ® TOLL HOUSE® Semi-Sweet
   Chocolate Morsels
1 cup chopped nuts
   Sweetened whipped cream or ice cream (optional)

BEAT eggs in large mixer bowl on high speed until foamy. Beat in
flour, granulated sugar and brown sugar. Beat in butter. Stir in
morsels and nuts. Spoon into pie shell.

BAKE in preheated 350°F. oven for 55 to 60 minutes or until knife
inserted halfway between outside edge and center comes out
clean. Cool on wire rack. Serve warm with whipped cream, if
desired. Makes 8 servings.

*NOTE: If using frozen pie shell, use a completely thawed deep-
dish style. Bake pie on heavy-duty baking sheet; increase baking
time slightly.

Chocolate Truffle Tart

CRUST:
- ⅔ cup all-purpose flour
- ½ cup powdered sugar
- ½ cup ground walnuts
- 6 tablespoons butter or margarine, softened
- ⅓ cup NESTLÉ® TOLL HOUSE® Baking Cocoa

FILLING:
- 1¼ cups heavy whipping cream
- ¼ cup granulated sugar
- 2 cups (12-ounce package) NESTLÉ® TOLL HOUSE® Semi-Sweet Chocolate Morsels
- 2 tablespoons seedless raspberry jam
  Sweetened whipped cream (optional)
  Fresh raspberries (optional)

For Crust:
BEAT flour, powdered sugar, walnuts, butter and cocoa in large mixer bowl until soft dough forms. Press dough into bottom and up side of ungreased 9- or 9½-inch fluted tart pan with removable bottom or 9-inch pie plate.

BAKE in preheated 350° oven for 12 to 14 minutes or until puffed. Cool completely in pan on wire rack.

For Filling:
COMBINE cream and sugar in medium, heavy-duty saucepan. Cook over medium heat, stirring occasionally, until mixture comes just to a boil. Remove from heat. Stir in morsels and jam; let stand for 5 minutes. Whisk until smooth. Transfer to medium mixer bowl. Cover; refrigerate for 45 to 60 minutes or until mixture is cooled and slightly thickened.

BEAT for 20 to 30 seconds or just until color lightens slightly. Spoon into crust. Refrigerate until firm. Remove side of pan; garnish, if desired, with whipped cream and raspberries. Makes 8 servings.

pies and tarts

Deep-Dish Peach Custard Pie

1 unbaked 9-inch (4-cup volume) deep-dish pie shell (see recipe, *page 194*)

7 medium peaches, peeled, pitted and sliced

1 can (14 ounces) NESTLÉ® CARNATION® Sweetened Condensed Milk

2 eggs

¼ cup (½ stick) butter or margarine, melted

1 to 3 teaspoons lemon juice

½ teaspoon ground cinnamon
   Dash ground nutmeg

⅓ cup packed brown sugar

⅓ cup all-purpose flour

⅓ cup chopped walnuts

2 tablespoons butter or margarine

ARRANGE peach slices in pie shell. Combine sweetened condensed milk, eggs, ¼ cup melted butter, lemon juice, cinnamon and nutmeg in large mixer bowl; beat until smooth. Pour over peaches. Bake in preheated 425°F. oven for 10 minutes.

COMBINE brown sugar, flour and walnuts in medium bowl. Cut in 2 tablespoons butter with pastry blender or 2 knives until mixture resembles coarse crumbs. Sprinkle mixture over pie.

REDUCE oven temperature to 350°F.; bake for additional 55 to 60 minutes or until knife inserted near center comes out clean. Cool on wire rack for 2 hours. Serve immediately or refrigerate. Makes 8 servings.

Pumpkin Cheese-Swirled Pie

1 unbaked 9-inch (4-cup volume) deep-dish pie shell (see recipe, *page 194*)

1 package (3 ounces) cream cheese, softened

½ cup light corn syrup, *divided*

½ teaspoon vanilla extract (optional)

1 cup LIBBY'S® 100% Pure Pumpkin

½ cup NESTLÉ® CARNATION® Evaporated Milk

2 eggs, lightly beaten

¼ cup granulated sugar

2 teaspoons pumpkin pie spice

¼ teaspoon salt

BEAT cream cheese in small mixer bowl until fluffy. Gradually add ¼ cup corn syrup and, if desired, vanilla extract; beat until smooth.

COMBINE pumpkin, evaporated milk, eggs, remaining corn syrup, sugar, pumpkin pie spice and salt in medium bowl. Pour into pie shell. Drop cream cheese mixture by rounded tablespoon onto pumpkin filling. Swirl mixture with spoon, pulling pumpkin mixture up to surface.

BAKE in preheated 325°F. oven for 50 to 60 minutes or until knife inserted near center comes out clean. Cool completely on wire rack. Makes 8 servings.

Pie Making Pointers

For custard-type pies that call for eggs and milk, use a wire whisk to thoroughly mix the filling ingredients.

Use glass or dull-finished aluminum pans for bottom crusts that are more crisp. If using shiny aluminum or foil pans, bake pies on preheated heavy-duty baking sheets.

Bake pies one at a time for even baking. If you need to bake two pies at once, stagger them on separate racks, then switch and rotate the pies halfway through baking.

If the edge of a pie crust starts to brown too quickly, cover it with strips of foil.

Pumpkin Dutch Apple Pie

1 unbaked 9-inch (4-cup volume) pie shell with high fluted edge (see recipe, *page 194*)

APPLE LAYER:

2 medium-size green apples, peeled, cored and thinly sliced (about 2 cups)

¾ cup granulated sugar, *divided*

2 teaspoons all-purpose flour

1 teaspoon lemon juice

¼ teaspoon ground cinnamon

PUMPKIN LAYER:

2 eggs

1½ cups LIBBY'S® 100% Pure Pumpkin

1 cup NESTLÉ® CARNATION® Evaporated Milk

2 tablespoons butter or margarine, melted

¾ teaspoon ground cinnamon

¼ teaspoon salt

⅛ teaspoon ground nutmeg

Crumble Topping (recipe follows)

For Apple Layer:
COMBINE apples with ¼ cup sugar, flour, lemon juice and cinnamon in medium bowl; place in pie shell.

For Pumpkin Layer:
COMBINE eggs, pumpkin, evaporated milk, remaining sugar, butter, cinnamon, salt and nutmeg in medium bowl; pour over apples.

BAKE in preheated 375° F. oven for 30 minutes. Remove from oven; sprinkle with Crumble Topping. Bake for 20 minutes more or until custard is set. Cool on wire rack. Makes 8 servings.

For Crumble Topping:
COMBINE ½ cup all-purpose flour, ⅓ cup chopped walnuts and 5 tablespoons granulated sugar in medium bowl. Cut in 3 tablespoons softened butter with pastry blender or 2 knives until crumbly.

Pictured on page 197.

Sour Cream Orange Pumpkin Pie

1 unbaked 9-inch (4-cup volume) deep-dish pie shell (see recipe, *page 194*)

2 eggs

1¾ cups (15-ounce can) LIBBY'S® 100% Pure Pumpkin

1 can (14 ounces) NESTLÉ® CARNATION® Sweetened Condensed Milk

1 tablespoon pumpkin pie spice

2 teaspoons grated orange peel

½ teaspoon salt

Sour Cream Orange Topping (recipe follows)

Orange slices, cut into wedges (optional)

COMBINE eggs, pumpkin, sweetened condensed milk, pumpkin pie spice, orange peel and salt in medium bowl; mix well. Pour into prepared pie shell.

BAKE in preheated 425°F. oven for 15 minutes. Reduce temperature to 350°F.; bake for 30 to 35 minutes or until knife inserted near center comes out clean. Cool pie for 10 minutes on wire rack.

SPREAD with Sour Cream Orange Topping; bake at 350°F. for 8 minutes. Cool on wire rack. If desired, garnish with orange wedges. Makes 8 servings.

For Sour Cream Orange Topping:
COMBINE 1¼ cups sour cream, 2 tablespoons granulated sugar, 2 teaspoons thawed frozen orange juice concentrate (or orange-flavored liqueur) and ½ teaspoon grated orange peel in small bowl.

NOTE: If using a metal or foil pan, bake pie on preheated, heavy-duty baking sheet.

Sour Cream Orange Pumpkin Pie (see recipe, above) and Pumpkin Cheesecake Tarts (see recipe, page 199)

Lite N' Easy Crustless Pumpkin Pie

2 tablespoons water

2 envelopes (7 grams each) unflavored gelatin

2¼ cups NESTLÉ® CARNATION® Evaporated Lowfat Milk, *divided*

1¾ cups (15-ounce can) LIBBY'S® 100% Pure Pumpkin

½ cup packed dark brown sugar or low calorie sweetener equivalent

2 teaspoons pumpkin pie spice

1 teaspoon vanilla extract

COAT 9-inch deep-dish pie plate with nonstick cooking spray.

PLACE water in medium bowl; sprinkle gelatin over water. Let stand for 5 to 10 minutes or until softened. Bring 1 cup evaporated milk just to a boil in small saucepan. Slowly stir hot evaporated milk into gelatin. Stir in remaining evaporated milk, pumpkin, brown sugar, pumpkin pie spice and vanilla extract.

POUR mixture into prepared pie plate. Refrigerate for 2 hours or until set. Makes 8 servings.

Libby's® Easy Pumpkin Cream Pie

1   prepared 9-inch (9 ounces) graham cracker crust
1¾ cups (15-ounce can) LIBBY'S® 100% Pure Pumpkin
1   package (5.1 ounces) vanilla instant pudding and pie
      filling mix
1   cup milk
1   teaspoon pumpkin pie spice
2   cups (about 6 ounces) frozen nondairy whipped topping,
      thawed, *divided*
      Fresh raspberries (optional)

COMBINE pumpkin, pudding mix, milk and pumpkin pie spice in
large mixer bowl; beat for 1 minute or until blended. Fold in
1½ cups whipped topping. Spoon into crust. Freeze for at least
4 hours or until firm. Let stand in refrigerator 1 hour before
serving. Garnish with remaining whipped topping and, if desired,
raspberries. Serve immediately. Makes 8 servings.

Homemade Pastry

1 cup all-purpose flour
½ teaspoon salt
6 tablespoons vegetable shortening
2 to 3 tablespoons cold water

MIX flour and salt in medium bowl; cut in shortening with pastry blender or 2 knives until crumbly. Gradually stir in cold water, mixing until flour is moistened.

SHAPE dough into ball; flatten to 1-inch thickness. On lightly floured board, roll dough into a circle about 2 inches larger than inverted 9-inch pie plate. Line pie plate with pastry. Trim pastry to ½ inch beyond the edge of the pie plate; fold extra pastry under and flute edge.

Note: Recipe can be doubled to make two 9-inch pie crusts or one double-crust 9-inch pie.

Secrets to Pastry Success

The first step to exceptional pies is tender, flaky pie crust. For perfect pastry you can brag about, follow this pie crust advice.

Measure the ingredients carefully. Too much flour makes the finished pie crust tough; too much shortening makes it crumbly.

Use a pastry blender or 2 knives to cut in the shortening so it is distributed evenly in the flour mixture and the mixture is crumbly.

Add the cold water gradually to the flour-shortening mixture and toss it together until the mixture is moistened evenly. Don't add too much water or your crust will be soggy or tough.

When it's time to roll out the crust, use as little flour as possible and roll the pastry to an even thickness. Adding too much flour at this step will make the crust tough, and a crust of uneven thickness will shrink excessively.

To transfer the pastry to the pie plate quickly and easily, wrap it around the rolling pin. Then, starting at one side of the pie plate, unroll the pastry into the plate. To avoid shrinkage of the crust as it bakes, don't stretch the pastry as you ease it into the plate.

Patch any cracks with a pastry scrap before adding the filling. Moisten the underside of the scrap with a little water so it stays in place.

Trim the pastry ½ inch beyond the rim of the pie plate and fold it under to build up the edge. For a fluted edge, place your index finger against the outside of the pastry; press the dough around your finger with your other hand's thumb and index finger.

Check that your oven temperature is accurate. If it is too low, the crust will be soggy. If it's too high, the pie won't bake evenly.

After baking, cool the pie on a wire rack. Allowing air to circulate under the pie as it cools keeps the pastry from becoming soggy.

If you don't have time to make pie pastry from scratch, use refrigerated pie crust, unbaked frozen pastry shells or pastry made from a pie crust mix instead of homemade pastry.

Macadamia Cheesecake Tart

CRUST:
- 1 cup chopped macadamia nuts
- 1 cup quick or old-fashioned oats
- 1 cup flaked coconut
- 2 tablespoons granulated sugar
- 7 tablespoons butter

FILLING:
- 1 package (8 ounces) cream cheese, softened
- ½ cup granulated sugar
- 2 eggs
- 1¾ cups (15-ounce can) LIBBY'S® 100% Pure Pumpkin
- 2 teaspoons ground cinnamon
- 1 teaspoon ground ginger
- 1 teaspoon vanilla extract
- Chopped macadamia nuts (optional)
- Toasted coconut (optional)

For Crust:

COMBINE macadamia nuts, oats, coconut and sugar in medium bowl. Cut in butter with pastry blender or 2 knives until blended. Press dough evenly into bottom and up sides of 11-inch tart pan with removable bottom. Bake in preheated 350°F. oven for 20 to 25 minutes or until lightly browned.

For Filling:

BEAT cream cheese and sugar in large mixer bowl until well blended. Add eggs, pumpkin, cinnamon, ginger and vanilla extract; blend well. Pour into baked crust.

BAKE at 350°F. for 35 to 40 minutes or until knife inserted near center comes out clean. Cool on wire rack. Refrigerate. Remove side of tart pan. Garnish, if desired, with additional macadamia nuts and coconut. Makes 14 servings.

Macadamia Cheesecake Tart (see recipe, above) and
Pumpkin Dutch Apple Pie (see recipe, page 189)

Chocolate Chip Fruit Tart

1 package (18 ounces) refrigerated NESTLÉ® TOLL HOUSE®
  Chocolate Chip Cookie Dough
1 package (8 ounces) cream cheese, softened
⅓ cup granulated sugar
½ teaspoon vanilla extract
1½ cups fruit (raspberries or blueberries and/or sliced kiwi,
  bananas, peaches or strawberries)

PRESS dough evenly into bottom and up sides of greased 9-inch
fluted tart pan with removable bottom.*

BAKE in preheated 350°F. oven for 18 to 20 minutes or until edge
is set and center is still slightly soft. Cool completely in pan on
wire rack.

BEAT cream cheese, sugar and vanilla extract in small mixer bowl
until smooth. Spread evenly over cooled cookie crust to within
½ inch of edge; arrange fruit as desired. Refrigerate for 1 hour.
Remove side of tart pan; slice into wedges. Makes 8 to 10 servings.

*Note: If tart pan is not available, press cookie dough onto greased
baking sheet into a 9- to 10-inch circle. Bake for 14 to 18 minutes.

Pumpkin Cheesecake Tarts

⅔ cup finely crushed gingersnap cookies (about 12 cookies)
2 tablespoons butter or margarine, melted
1 package (8 ounces) cream cheese, softened
1 cup LIBBY'S® 100% Pure Pumpkin
½ cup granulated sugar
1 teaspoon pumpkin pie spice
1 teaspoon vanilla extract
2 eggs
2 tablespoons sour cream
2 tablespoons NESTLÉ® TOLL HOUSE® Semi-Sweet Chocolate Morsels

COMBINE crushed gingersnap cookies and butter in small bowl. Press scant tablespoon cookie mixture onto bottom of each of 12 paper-lined muffin cups. Bake in preheated 325°F. oven for 5 minutes.

BEAT cream cheese, pumpkin, sugar, pumpkin pie spice and vanilla extract in small mixer bowl until blended. Add eggs; beat well. Pour into muffin cups, filling ¾ full.

BAKE at 325°F. for 25 to 30 minutes or until set. Cool in pan on wire rack. Remove tarts from pan; chill.

GARNISH with sour cream. Place morsels in small, heavy-duty plastic bag. Microwave on HIGH (100%) power for 20 seconds, knead bag to mix. Microwave at additional 10-second intervals, kneading until smooth. Cut a small hole in corner of bag; squeeze to drizzle chocolate over tarts. Makes 1 dozen tarts.

Pictured on page 191.

Crumb-Topped Pumpkin Pear Tart

PEAR LAYER:

   Pastry for single crust pie (see recipe, *page 194*)
2 medium-size pears, peeled, cored and thinly sliced (about 2 cups)
2 tablespoons granulated sugar
2 teaspoons all-purpose flour
¼ teaspoon ground cinnamon

PUMPKIN LAYER:

2 eggs
1½ cups LIBBY'S® 100% Pure Pumpkin
1 cup NESTLÉ® CARNATION® Evaporated Milk
½ cup granulated sugar
2 tablespoons butter or margarine, melted
¾ teaspoon ground cinnamon
¼ teaspoon salt
⅛ teaspoon ground nutmeg
   Crumb Topping (recipe follows)

For Pear Layer:

PLACE pastry in a 10- or 11-inch tart pan with removable bottom (or a 9-inch pie plate). Trim excess pastry.* Combine pears with sugar, flour and cinnamon in medium bowl; place in tart shell.

For Pumpkin Layer:

COMBINE eggs, pumpkin, evaporated milk, sugar, butter, cinnamon, salt and nutmeg in bowl; pour mixture over pears. Bake in preheated 375°F. oven 25 minutes (30 minutes for pie plate). Remove from oven; sprinkle with Crumb Topping. Bake tart 15 minutes more (20 minutes for pie plate) or until custard is set. Cool. Remove side of tart pan. Makes 10 servings.

For Crumb Topping:

COMBINE ½ cup all-purpose flour, ⅓ cup chopped walnuts and 5 tablespoons granulated sugar in medium bowl. Cut in 3 tablespoons softened butter or margarine with pastry blender or 2 knives until crumbly.

*Note: If desired, cut pastry scraps into decorative designs; place on an ungreased baking sheet. Brush with beaten egg. Bake in 375°F. oven 10 minutes or until golden. Place on baked tart.

Pumpkin Meringue Tarts

MERINGUE TARTS:

  3 egg whites

 ½ teaspoon cream of tartar

 ¼ teaspoon salt

 ¾ cup granulated sugar

     Ground cinnamon (optional)

FILLING:

  1 package (4-serving size) instant sugar-free vanilla pudding

1½ cups low-fat or nonfat milk

  1 cup LIBBY'S® 100% Pure Pumpkin

  1 teaspoon ground cinnamon

For Meringue Tarts:

BEAT egg whites, cream of tartar and salt in small mixer bowl on high speed until soft peaks form. Gradually add sugar, beating on high speed until stiff peaks form. Spoon mixture onto lightly greased baking sheets (or use pastry bag with star tip), forming eight 4-inch round or oval "nests."

BAKE in preheated 300°F. oven for 30 to 35 minutes or until crisp. Cool on baking sheets for 5 minutes; remove to wire racks to cool completely. If desired, sprinkle lightly with ground cinnamon.

For Filling:

BEAT pudding and milk according to package directions; refrigerate for 5 minutes. Add pumpkin and 1 teaspoon cinnamon; mix well. Chill for 10 minutes. Spoon filling (or use pastry bag with star tip) into meringue tarts. Serve immediately. Makes 8 tarts.

brunch dishes, muffins & more

greet the day with fresh-from the-oven muffins, hearty brunch casseroles or pancakes hot off the griddle. Hosting a weekend brunch? Build a menu around Pumpkin Streusel Coffee Cake and cheesy Sausage Breakfast Casserole or classic Quiche Lorraine. During the week, send the family off with easy-to-make Pumpkin Oatmeal or Toasted Almond Muffins.

Hash Brown Casserole (see recipe, page 228), Blueberry White Chip Muffins (see recipe, page 206), and Pumpkin Chocolate Chip Muffins (see recipe, page 207).

Blueberry White Chip Muffins

2¼ cups all-purpose flour, *divided*
½ cup plus ⅓ cup granulated sugar, *divided*
¼ cup packed brown sugar
2½ teaspoons baking powder
½ teaspoon salt
¾ cup milk
1 egg, lightly beaten
¼ cup (½ stick) butter or margarine, melted
½ teaspoon grated lemon peel
2 cups (12-ounce package) NESTLÉ® TOLL HOUSE® Premier White Morsels, *divided*
1½ cups fresh or frozen blueberries
¼ teaspoon ground cinnamon
3 tablespoons butter or margarine

COMBINE 2 cups flour, ½ cup granulated sugar, brown sugar, baking powder and salt in large bowl. Stir in milk, egg, ¼ cup melted butter and lemon peel. Stir in 1½ cups morsels and blueberries. Spoon into 18 greased or paper-lined muffin cups, filling almost full.

COMBINE remaining flour, remaining granulated sugar and cinnamon in small bowl. Cut in 3 tablespoons butter with pastry blender or 2 knives until mixture resembles coarse crumbs. Sprinkle over batter in muffin cups.

BAKE in preheated 375°F. oven for 22 to 25 minutes or until wooden pick inserted in centers comes out clean. Cool in pans for 5 minutes; remove to wire racks to cool slightly.

PLACE remaining morsels in small, heavy-duty plastic bag. Microwave on MEDIUM-HIGH (70%) power for 30 seconds; knead. Microwave at additional 10- to 20-second intervals, kneading until smooth. Cut tiny corner from bag; squeeze to drizzle over muffins. Serve warm. Makes 1½ dozen muffins.

Pictured on pages 204 and 205.

Pumpkin Chocolate Chip Muffins

3 cups all-purpose flour
1 cup granulated sugar
1 tablespoon baking powder
1 teaspoon salt
1 teaspoon ground cinnamon
2 eggs
1¼ cups LIBBY'S® 100% Pure Pumpkin
1¾ cups milk
½ cup (1 stick) butter, melted
1½ cups (9 ounces) NESTLÉ® TOLL HOUSE® Semi-Sweet
    Chocolate Morsels
1 cup finely chopped walnuts, *divided*

COMBINE flour, sugar, baking powder, salt and cinnamon in medium bowl.

BEAT eggs lightly in large bowl. Mix in pumpkin, milk and butter. Stir in morsels and ½ cup nuts. Stir in flour mixture just until moistened. Spoon batter into 24 greased or paper-lined muffin cups, filling almost full. Sprinkle with remaining nuts.

BAKE in preheated 400°F. oven for 20 to 25 minutes. Cool for 5 minutes; remove from pan. Serve warm. Makes 2 dozen muffins.

Pictured on pages 204 and 205.

Special Uses for Extra Pumpkin:

If your recipe calls for less than a whole can of pumpkin (about 1¾ cups), save the rest and try one of these quick ideas.

Whisk pumpkin into soups and sauces. It will add flavor and nutrients.

Stir pumpkin into mashed potatoes for a fall-color favorite.

Stir pumpkin into softened ice cream for a new dessert idea. Try vanilla, caramel swirl or butter pecan flavors.

Mix pumpkin with prepared (and partially set up) vanilla or butterscotch pudding.

Create a sauce for pancakes or waffles by mixing pumpkin with maple syrup, brown sugar or honey, and cinnamon.

Pumpkin Blueberry Streusel Muffins

2½ cups all-purpose flour
2 cups granulated sugar
1 tablespoon pumpkin pie spice
1 teaspoon baking soda
½ teaspoon salt
2 eggs
1 cup LIBBY'S® 100% Pure Pumpkin
½ cup vegetable oil
1 cup fresh or frozen blueberries
Streusel Topping (recipe follows)

COMBINE flour, sugar, pumpkin pie spice, baking soda and salt in large bowl. Combine eggs, pumpkin and oil in medium bowl; stir into flour mixture just until moistened. Fold in blueberries. Spoon batter into 18 greased or paper-lined muffin cups, filling ¾ full. Sprinkle with Streusel Topping.

BAKE in preheated 350°F. oven for 30 to 35 minutes or until wooden pick inserted in centers comes out clean. Cool in pans on wire racks. Makes 1½ dozen muffins.

For Streusel Topping:
COMBINE ⅓ cup granulated sugar, 3 tablespoons all-purpose flour and ½ teaspoon ground cinnamon in medium bowl. Cut in 2 tablespoons butter with pastry blender or 2 knives until mixture is crumbly.

Pumpkin Corn Muffins

1¼ cups all-purpose flour
1 cup ALBERS® Yellow Corn Meal
⅓ cup granulated sugar
4 teaspoons baking powder
½ teaspoon salt
1¼ cups LIBBY'S® 100% Pure Pumpkin
2 eggs
⅓ cup milk
¼ cup vegetable oil

COMBINE flour, corn meal, sugar, baking powder and salt in large bowl. Beat pumpkin, eggs, milk and vegetable oil in medium bowl. Add to flour mixture; mix well. Spoon into 12 greased or paper-lined muffin cups. Bake in preheated 375°F. oven for 25 to 30 minutes or until wooden pick inserted in center comes out clean. Remove to wire rack; cool slightly. Serve warm. Makes 1 dozen muffins.

Pictured on page 211.

Mighty Good Muffins

Go ahead and splurge! Treat yourself to warm muffins right from the oven. To help you bake the best muffins possible, remember these helpful suggestions:

Use a light hand when you mix the muffin batter. If you overmix, the muffins may have peaked tops, tunnels inside and a tough texture.

Avoid crusty rims around the edges of muffins by greasing the muffin cups on the bottoms and only halfway up the sides.

Muffins are done when they have golden tops and a wooden pick inserted in the center comes out clean. Remove to wire rack; cool slightly.

Store cooled muffins in a plastic bag at room temperature for up to 3 days. Or, place them in freezer bags and freeze for up to 3 months. To reheat frozen muffins, wrap them in foil and bake in a 300°F. oven for 12 to 15 minutes for 1¾-inch muffins or 15 to 18 minutes for 2½-inch ones.

brunch dishes, muffins & more

Orange Brunch Muffins

3 cups buttermilk baking mix
¾ cup all-purpose flour
⅔ cup granulated sugar
2 eggs, lightly beaten
½ cup plain yogurt
½ cup orange juice
1 tablespoon grated orange peel
2 cups (12-ounce package) NESTLÉ® TOLL HOUSE® Premier White Morsels, *divided*
½ cup chopped macadamia nuts or walnuts

COMBINE baking mix, flour and sugar in large bowl. Add eggs, yogurt, orange juice and orange peel; stir just until blended. Stir in 1⅓ cups morsels. Spoon into 12 to 14 paper-lined muffin cups. Sprinkle with nuts.

BAKE in preheated 375°F. oven for 18 to 22 minutes or until wooden pick inserted in center comes out clean. Cool in pans on wire rack for 10 minutes; remove to wire rack to cool lightly.

PLACE remaining morsels in small, heavy-duty plastic bag. Microwave on MEDIUM-HIGH (70%) power for 1 minute; knead bag to mix. Microwave at additional 10- to 20- second intervals, kneading until smooth. Cut a small hole in corner of bag; squeeze to drizzle chocolate over muffins while still slightly warm. Serve warm. Makes 12 to 14 muffins.

Toasted Almond Muffins

2½ cups all-purpose baking mix
1 can (12 fluid ounces) NESTLÉ® CARNATION®
  Evaporated Milk
1 cup granulated sugar
⅓ cup vegetable oil
1 egg
1 cup sliced almonds, toasted, *divided*
1 cup sifted powdered sugar
1 to 2 tablespoons orange juice

COMBINE baking mix, evaporated milk, granulated sugar, vegetable oil and egg in large mixer bowl. Beat on high speed for 30 seconds or until blended. Fold in ¾ cup nuts. Spoon batter into 18 greased paper-lined muffin cups, filling ⅔ full.

BAKE in preheated 375°F. oven for 15 to 18 minutes or until wooden pick inserted in centers comes out clean. Remove to wire racks to cool completely.

COMBINE powdered sugar and orange juice in small bowl. Spread over each muffin; sprinkle with remaining nuts. Makes 1½ dozen muffins.

Pumpkin Apple Dessert Pizza

1 roll (18 ounces) refrigerated sugar cookie dough
1 cup LIBBY'S® 100% Pure Pumpkin
1 package (3 ounces) cream cheese, softened
3 tablespoons granulated sugar, *divided*
½ teaspoon ground cinnamon
1 medium green apple, peeled, cored and thinly sliced (about 1 cup)
  Dash ground cinnamon
⅓ cup chopped walnuts
1 to 2 tablespoons caramel-flavored ice cream topping

FREEZE cookie dough for 30 minutes; slice into ¼-inch-thick pieces (about 32). Place slices, edges touching, on greased 12-inch pizza pan.* Bake in preheated 350°F. oven for 12 to 15 minutes or until golden brown. Remove from oven; prick with fork. Cool on wire rack.

BEAT pumpkin, cream cheese, 2 tablespoons sugar and ½ teaspoon cinnamon in small mixer bowl until smooth. Spread over pizza crust to within ¾ inch of edge. Mix apple slices with remaining sugar and dash cinnamon in small bowl; place on pizza. Sprinkle with walnuts.

BAKE at 350°F. for 8 minutes more. Place on wire rack. Drizzle with caramel topping. Cool slightly. Cut into wedges; serve warm. Makes 12 servings.

*NOTE: Recipe also may be made in 13 x 9-inch baking pan. Bake crust in preheated 350°F. oven for 15 to 17 minutes or until golden brown. Add apple topping and bake for 10 minutes more.

Pumpkin Turnovers

PASTRY:

2½ cups all-purpose flour

2 tablespoons granulated sugar

1 teaspoon salt

½ teaspoon ground cinnamon

½ cup (1 stick) butter or margarine, melted

½ cup milk

1 egg

FILLING:

1¾ cup (15-ounce can) LIBBY'S® 100% Pure Pumpkin

¾ cup packed brown sugar

¾ cup chopped pecans or walnuts

½ cup raisins

1 tablespoon lemon juice

1 tablespoon water

1 teaspoon ground cinnamon

⅛ teaspoon ground cloves

1 egg, lightly beaten

Cinnamon Sugar (recipe follows)

For Pastry:

COMBINE flour, granulated sugar, salt and cinnamon in medium bowl. Beat butter, milk and egg in small bowl until combined. Add to flour mixture; mix well. Form into ball. Cover; refrigerate for 1 hour.

For Filling:

COMBINE pumpkin and brown sugar in medium bowl. Add pecans, raisins, lemon juice, water, cinnamon and cloves; mix well.

DIVIDE pastry into 12 to 14 portions. On lightly floured board, roll each portion into 6-inch circle. Place scant ¼ cup filling on each circle. Moisten edges with water; fold in half, pressing edges with fork to seal. Scallop sealed edges by indenting with the handle of fork at ¾-inch intervals. Place on ungreased baking sheet. Brush egg over tops of turnovers. Sprinkle with Cinnamon Sugar.

BAKE in preheated 400°F. oven for 15 to 20 minutes or until golden brown. Serve warm or cool on wire rack. Makes 12 to 14 turnovers.

For Cinnamon Sugar:

COMBINE ¼ cup granulated sugar and 1 teaspoon ground cinnamon in small bowl.

Toll House® Crumb Cake

TOPPING:

- ⅓ cup packed brown sugar
- 1 tablespoon all-purpose flour
- 2 tablespoons butter or margarine
- ½ cup chopped nuts
- 2 cups (12-ounce package) NESTLÉ® TOLL HOUSE® Semi-Sweet Chocolate Morsels, *divided*

CAKE:

- 1¾ cups all-purpose flour
- 1 teaspoon baking powder
- 1 teaspoon baking soda
- ¼ teaspoon salt
- ¾ cup granulated sugar
- ½ cup (1 stick) butter or margarine, softened
- 1 teaspoon vanilla extract
- 3 eggs
- 1 cup sour cream

For Topping:

COMBINE brown sugar, flour and butter in small bowl with pastry blender or 2 knives until crumbly. Stir in nuts and ½ cup morsels.

For Cake:

COMBINE flour, baking powder, baking soda and salt in small bowl. Beat sugar, butter and vanilla extract in large mixer bowl until creamy. Add eggs, one at a time, beating well after each addition. Gradually add flour mixture alternately with sour cream. Fold in remaining morsels. Spread into greased 13 x 9-inch baking pan; sprinkle with topping.

BAKE in preheated 350°F. oven for 25 to 35 minutes or until wooden pick inserted in center comes out clean. Cool in pan on wire rack. Makes 12 servings.

Pumpkin Oatmeal Spice Tortes

1¾ cups (15-ounce can) LIBBY'S® 100% Pure Pumpkin
¾ cup packed brown sugar
1½ teaspoons ground cinnamon
1 package (18¼ ounces) spice cake mix
2 eggs
½ cup (1 stick) butter or margarine, softened
Oatmeal Topping (recipe follows)

COMBINE pumpkin, brown sugar and cinnamon in medium bowl.

COMBINE cake mix, eggs and butter in large mixer bowl; beat on low speed until blended (batter will be stiff). Spread into 2 greased 9-inch round cake pans.

BAKE in preheated 350°F. oven for 15 minutes; remove from oven. Spread with pumpkin mixture; sprinkle with Oatmeal Topping. Return to oven; bake for 15 minutes more. Cool in pans on wire racks. Makes 12 servings.

For Oatmeal Topping:
COMBINE 1 cup quick or old-fashioned oats, ¾ cup packed brown sugar, ½ cup chopped walnuts, ¼ cup melted butter or margarine and 1 teaspoon ground cinnamon.

Measuring Oats

Measure quick or old-fashioned oats as you do flour by spooning the oats into a dry measuring cup, then leveling with a straight-edged spatula. If you use the scoop-and-shake method, you will use more oats than necessary, which causes a dry topping, cookie or cake.

Toll House® Mini Morsel Pancakes

2½ cups all-purpose flour
1 cup (6 ounces) NESTLÉ® TOLL HOUSE® Semi-Sweet
    Chocolate Mini Morsels
1 tablespoon baking powder
½ teaspoon salt
1¾ cups milk
2 eggs
⅓ cup vegetable oil
⅓ cup packed brown sugar
    Powdered sugar
    Strawberries

COMBINE flour, morsels, baking powder and salt in large bowl. Combine milk, eggs, vegetable oil and brown sugar in medium bowl; add to flour mixture. Stir just until moistened; batter may be lumpy.

HEAT griddle or skillet over medium heat; brush lightly with vegetable oil. Pour ¼ cup batter per pancake onto hot griddle; cook until bubbles begin to burst. Turn and cook about 1 minute longer or until golden. Repeat with remaining batter.

SPRINKLE with powdered sugar; top with strawberries. Makes about 18 pancakes.

Nutty Pumpkin Waffles

2 cups all-purpose flour
¼ cup granulated sugar
1 tablespoon cornstarch
2 teaspoons baking powder
2 teaspoons ground cinnamon
½ teaspoon salt
¼ teaspoon ground ginger
¼ teaspoon ground nutmeg
1¾ cups milk
½ cup LIBBY'S® 100% Pure Pumpkin
2 eggs, separated
2 tablespoons butter or margarine, melted
¾ cup chopped nuts
Pumpkin Maple Sauce (recipe follows)
Chopped nuts

COMBINE flour, sugar, cornstarch, baking powder, cinnamon, salt, ginger and nutmeg in large bowl. Combine milk, pumpkin and egg yolks in medium bowl; mix well. Add to flour mixture. Stir in butter. Beat egg whites in small mixer bowl on high speed until soft peaks form. Gently fold into pumpkin mixture.

PREHEAT waffle iron according to manufacturer's directions. Depending on size of waffle iron, pour ½ to 1½ cups batter onto hot iron. Generously sprinkle with nuts. Cook for 4 to 5 minutes or until steaming stops. Repeat with remaining batter and nuts. Serve with Pumpkin Maple Sauce. Sprinkle with additional nuts. Makes eight 7-inch waffles.

For Pumpkin Maple Sauce:
HEAT 1 cup maple syrup, ¾ cup LIBBY'S® 100% Pure Pumpkin and ¼ teaspoon ground cinnamon in small saucepan until warm.

Hash Brown Casserole

2 cups (8 ounces) shredded cheddar cheese
3 cartons (4 ounces each) cholesterol-free egg product or
   6 eggs, well beaten
1 can (12 fluid ounces) NESTLÉ® CARNATION®
   Evaporated Milk
1 teaspoon salt
½ teaspoon ground black pepper
1 package (26 ounces) frozen shredded hash brown potatoes
1 medium onion, chopped
1 small green bell pepper, chopped
1 cup diced ham (optional)

COMBINE cheese, egg product, evaporated milk, salt and black pepper in large bowl. Add potatoes, onion, bell pepper and, if desired, ham; mix well. Pour mixture into greased 13 x 9-inch baking dish.

BAKE in preheated 350°F. oven for 60 to 65 minutes or until set. Makes 12 servings.

Pictured on pages 204 and 205.

Breakfast Sausage Casserole

  1 package (16 ounces) bulk pork sausage, cooked, drained and crumbled

  4 cups cubed day-old bread

  2 cups (8 ounces) shredded sharp cheddar cheese

  2 cans (12 ounces each) NESTLÉ® CARNATION® Evaporated Milk

10 eggs, lightly beaten

  1 teaspoon dry mustard

  ¼ teaspoon onion powder

     Ground black pepper

PLACE bread in greased 13 x 9-inch baking dish. Sprinkle with cheese. Combine evaporated milk, eggs, dry mustard, onion powder and black pepper to taste in medium bowl. Pour evenly over bread and cheese. Sprinkle with sausage. Cover; refrigerate overnight.

BAKE in preheated 325°F. oven for 55 to 60 minutes or until cheese is golden brown. Cover with foil if top browns too quickly. Makes 6 servings.

Quiche Lorraine

1 unbaked 9-inch (4-cup volume) deep-dish pie shell (see recipe, *page 194*)
6 slices bacon, cut up
½ cup chopped onion
1½ cups (6 ounces) shredded Swiss cheese
1 can (12 fluid ounces) NESTLÉ® CARNATION® Evaporated Milk
3 eggs, well beaten
¼ teaspoon salt
⅛ teaspoon ground black pepper
⅛ teaspoon ground nutmeg
   Crumbled cooked bacon (optional)
   Snipped chives (optional)

COOK 6 slices bacon in large skillet over medium heat. When bacon starts to turn brown, add onion. Cook until bacon is crisp; drain. Sprinkle cheese into bottom of pie shell. Top with bacon mixture. Combine evaporated milk, eggs, salt, black pepper and nutmeg in small bowl until blended. Pour into pie shell.*

BAKE in preheated 350°F. oven for 30 to 35 minutes or until knife inserted halfway between center and edge comes out clean. Let cool for 5 minutes before serving. If desired, garnish with crumbled bacon and chives. Makes 8 servings.

*Note: If using metal or foil pans, bake quiche on preheated heavy-duty baking sheet.

Plan a Brunch Bash

A brunch bash is an ideal way to entertain family and friends for the holidays. Schedule your brunch anytime from mid-morning to early afternoon. For the menu, mix and match the recipes in this chapter and include some fresh fruit or an assortment of fruit juices. For a large group, serve brunch buffet style; for smaller numbers, plan a sit-down meal.

Pumpkin Apple Butter

1 can (15 ounces) LIBBY'S® 100% Pure Pumpkin
1 cup (about 1 medium) apple peeled, cored and grated
1 cup apple juice
½ cup packed brown sugar
¾ teaspoon pumpkin pie spice

COMBINE pumpkin, apple, apple juice, brown sugar and pumpkin pie spice in medium, heavy-duty saucepan. Bring to a boil; reduce heat to low. Cook, stirring occasionally, for 1½ hours. Serve with buttermilk biscuits, breads, corn muffins or hot cereal. Store in airtight container in refrigerator for up to 2 months. Makes 3 cups.

Sweet Pumpkin Dip

2   packages (8 ounces each) cream cheese, softened
1   can (15 ounces) LIBBY'S® 100% Pure Pumpkin
2   cups sifted powdered sugar
1   teaspoon ground cinnamon
1   teaspoon ground ginger
    Sliced fruit, bite-size cinnamon graham crackers, toasted
    mini-bagels, toast slices, muffins or English muffins

BEAT cream cheese and pumpkin in large mixer bowl until smooth. Add powdered sugar, cinnamon and ginger; mix thoroughly. Cover; refrigerate for 1 hour. Serve as a dip or spread. Makes about 5½ cups.

baking basics

If you know the basics, you can master the skill of baking. Here are some baking tips, plus step-by-step instructions for melting chocolate, that will help you bake and decorate everything from the simplest cookies to the most elaborate desserts.

butter & margarine

For baking, the Nestlé Culinary Center suggests using butter or regular stick margarine for the best results. However, if you prefer using a lower-fat margarine, choose one with no less than 60% vegetable oil. Products labeled as "spread" and "diet" contain less fat and more water. They tend to produce a cookie that is more cakelike and less crisp around the edges.

masterful melting

The key to melting chocolate successfully is to use slow and gentle heat.

Melting Larger Amounts

To melt NESTLÉ® TOLL HOUSE® Semi-Sweet Chocolate Morsels or broken-up Semi-Sweet or Unsweetened Chocolate Baking Bars, microwave 1 cup (6 ounces) in an uncovered microwave-safe bowl on HIGH (100%) power for 1 minute; stir. Microwave at additional 10- to 20-second intervals, stirring until smooth.

For the more delicate products—Milk Chocolate Morsels, Butterscotch Morsels, Premier White Morsels or Premier White Baking Bars—melt as above, except use MEDIUM-HIGH (70%) power.

Or, melt morsels or baking bars in a *heavy-duty* saucepan on *lowest possible* heat. When chocolate begins to melt and become shiny, remove from heat; stir. Return to heat for a few seconds at a time, stirring until smooth. (This method is not recommended for more delicate morsels and baking bars.)

Dazzle with a Drizzle

A drizzle of white "chocolate" adds a pastry-shop touch to cookies, brownies, cakes, fudge and truffles. Place ½ cup NESTLÉ® TOLL HOUSE® Premier White Morsels or 2 bars (2 ounces *each*) NESTLÉ® TOLL HOUSE® Premier White Baking Bar in a heavy-duty plastic bag. Microwave on MEDIUM-HIGH (70%) power for 45 seconds; knead bag to mix. Microwave at additional 10- to 20-second intervals, kneading until smooth. (Semi-sweet chocolate morsels and baking bars may be melted in the same way, using HIGH (100%) power.)

Cut a small hole in the corner of the bag; squeeze to drizzle. For a thicker or thinner drizzle, adjust the size of the hole you cut in the bag.

equipment

Use these tips when considering mixing equipment and bakeware:

Consider a portable electric mixer (hand-held mixer) for light jobs and short mixing periods. For heavy-duty jobs and long mixing periods, use a freestanding electric mixer.

The material bakeware is made from—aluminum, tin, stainless steel, black steel or pottery—and the finish it has influence the quality of baked products. Shiny bakeware reflects heat, making the browning process slower, while dark bakeware and bakeware with a dull finish absorb more heat, increasing browning of baked goods.

measuring

Not all ingredients are measured the same way, so keep this measuring guide handy when baking:

Measuring spoons are different from the ones you use for eating. Generally, these spoons come in a set that includes 1-tablespoon, 1-teaspoon, ½-teaspoon and ¼-teaspoon sizes. Use measuring spoons to measure small amounts of both liquid and dry ingredients.

When measuring liquids of ¼ cup or larger, use a standard glass or clear plastic liquid measuring cup. Place the cup on a level surface; bend down so your eye is level with the marking you wish to read. Fill the cup up to the marking. Do not lift the cup off the counter to your eye while measuring; your hand is not as steady as the countertop.

When measuring dry ingredients, use a dry measuring cup that is the exact capacity you wish to measure. These individual cups usually come in sets, including 1-cup, ½-cup, ⅓-cup and ¼-cup sizes. Using a spoon, lightly pile the ingredient into the cup. Then, using a metal spatula, level off the measure. Never pack dry ingredients except brown sugar. Pack brown sugar into the cup so it holds the shape of the measuring cup.

Is sifting necessary? All-purpose flour is no longer lumpy and compact like the flour of yesteryear. That's why stirring it before measuring is sufficient. Stirring works well for most other flours also, except cake flour, which has a very soft texture and tends to pack down. We recommend that you sift cake flour to remove any lumps and to lighten it before measuring.

A dash is a measure of less than ⅛ teaspoon. To get a dash, just add a quick shake or a sprinkle of the ingredient. When a dash is used, it's usually for flavor; the actual amount is up to you.

oven tips

When monitoring oven temperature, use an oven thermometer. Since temperature variances of up to 25°F. are quite common, it's a good idea to check the internal temperature of your oven before baking. If the temperature is too high or low, adjust the settings accordingly.

Preheating the oven will give you the best results when making baked goods. All recipe timings in this cookbook are based on a preheated oven.

If the appearance or texture of a baked product does not seem correct, review the oven manufacturer's instructions for the proper procedure in preheating your oven. Also, after preheating your oven, double-check the oven's internal temperature with an oven thermometer.

index

index

metric cooking hints

Metric Cooking Hints

By making a few conversions, cooks in Australia, Canada, and the United Kingdom can use the recipes in *Nestlé® All-Time Favorite Cookie and Baking Recipes* with confidence. The charts on this page provide a guide for converting measurements from the U.S. customary system, which is used throughout this book, to the imperial and metric systems. There also is a conversion table for oven temperatures to accommodate the differences in oven calibrations.

Product Differences: Most of the ingredients called for in the recipes in this book are available in English-speaking countries. However, some are known by different names. Here are some common American ingredients and their possible counterparts:
- Sugar is granulated or castor sugar.
- Powdered sugar is icing sugar.
- All-purpose flour is plain household flour or white flour. When self-rising flour is used in place of all-purpose flour in a recipe that calls for leavening, omit the leavening agent (baking soda or baking powder) and salt.
- Light corn syrup is golden syrup.
- Cornstarch is cornflour.
- Baking soda is bicarbonate of soda.
- Vanilla is vanilla essence.
- Green, red, or yellow sweet peppers are capsicums.
- Golden raisins are sultanas.

Volume and Weight: Americans traditionally use cup measures for liquid and solid ingredients. The chart, below, shows the approximate imperial and metric equivalents. If you are accustomed to weighing solid ingredients, the following approximate equivalents will be helpful.
- 1 cup butter, castor sugar, or rice = 8 ounces = about 250 grams
- 1 cup flour = 4 ounces = about 125 grams
- 1 cup icing sugar = 5 ounces = about 150 grams

Spoon measures are used for smaller amounts of ingredients. Although the size of the tablespoon varies slightly in different countries, for practical purposes and for recipes in this book, a straight substitution is all that's necessary.

Measurements made using cups or spoons always should be level unless stated otherwise.

Equivalents: U.S. = Australia/U.K.

⅛ teaspoon = 0.5 ml
¼ teaspoon = 1 ml
½ teaspoon = 2 ml
1 teaspoon = 5 ml
1 tablespoon = 1 tablespoon
¼ cup = 2 tablespoons = 2 fluid ounces = 60 ml
⅓ cup = ¼ cup = 3 fluid ounces = 90 ml
½ cup = ⅓ cup = 4 fluid ounces = 120 ml
⅔ cup = ½ cup = 5 fluid ounces = 150 ml
¾ cup = ⅔ cup = 6 fluid ounces = 180 ml
1 cup = ¾ cup = 8 fluid ounces = 240 ml
1¼ cups = 1 cup
2 cups = 1 pint
1 quart = 1 liter
½ inch = 1.27 cm
1 inch = 2.54 cm

Baking Pan Sizes

American	Metric
8 x 1½-inch round baking pan	20 x 4-cm cake tin
9 x 1½-inch round baking pan	23 x 3.5-cm cake tin
11 x 7 x 1½-inch baking pan	28 x 18 x 4-cm baking tin
13 x 9 x 2-inch baking pan	30 x 20 x 3-cm baking tin
2-quart rectangular baking dish	30 x 20 x 3-cm baking tin
15 x 10 x 1-inch baking pan	30 x 25 x 2-cm baking tin (Swiss roll tin)
9-inch pie plate	22 x 4- or 23 x 4-cm pie plate
7- or 8-inch springform pan	18- or 20-cm springform or loose-bottom cake tin
9 x 5 x 3-inch loaf pan	23 x 13 x 7-cm or 2-pound narrow loaf tin or pâté tin
1½-quart casserole	1.5-liter casserole
2-quart casserole	2-liter casserole

Oven Temperature Equivalents

Fahrenheit Setting	Celsius Setting*	Gas Setting
300°F	150°C	Gas Mark 2 (slow)
325°F	160°C	Gas Mark 3 (moderately slow)
350°F	180°C	Gas Mark 4 (moderate)
375°F	190°C	Gas Mark 5 (moderately hot)
400°F	200°C	Gas Mark 6 (hot)
425°F	220°C	Gas Mark 7
450°F	230°C	Gas Mark 8 (very hot)
Broil		Grill

*Electric and gas ovens may be calibrated using Celsius. However, for an electric oven, increase the Celsius setting 10 to 20 degrees when cooking above 160°C. For convection or forced-air ovens (gas or electric), lower the temperature setting 10°C when cooking at all heat levels.